Caring for Clergy

Caring for Clergy

Understanding a Disconnected Network of Providers

Thad S. Austin *and* Katie R. Comeau

Foreword by Christopher J. Adams

CASCADE *Books* · Eugene, Oregon

CARING FOR CLERGY
Understanding a Disconnected Network of Providers

Cascade Books
An Imprint of Wipf and Stock Publishers
199 W. 8th Ave., Suite 3
Eugene, OR 97401

www.wipfandstock.com

PAPERBACK ISBN: 978-1-6667-4153-7
HARDCOVER ISBN: 978-1-6667-4154-4
EBOOK ISBN: 978-1-6667-4155-1

Cataloguing-in-Publication data:

Names: Austin, Thad D., author. | Comeau, Katie R., author. | Adams, Christopher J., foreword.

Title: Caring for clergy : understanding a disconnected netework of providers / Thad S. Austin and Katie R. Comeau ; foreword by Christopher J. Adams.

Description: Eugene, OR : Cascade Books, 2022 | Includes bibliographical references.

Identifiers: ISBN 978-1-6667-4153-7 (paperback) | ISBN 978-1-6667-4154-4 (hardcover) | ISBN 978-1-6667-4155-1 (ebook)

Subjects: LCSH: Clergy—Job stress. | Clergy. | Stress, Physiological.

Classification: BV4398 .C27 2022 (print) | BV4398 .C27 (ebook)

07/12/22

To all those who lift the arms of clergy

Whenever Moses held up his hand, Israel would start winning the battle. Whenever Moses lowered his hand, Amalek would start winning. But Moses' hands grew tired. So they took a stone and put it under Moses so he could sit down on it. Aaron and Hur held up his hands, one on each side of him so that his hands remained steady until sunset.

Exod 17:11–12, CEB

Research Team

Principal Investigator and Co-Author
Rev. Thad S. Austin, PhD

Co-Author and Post-Doctoral Fellow
Katie R. Comeau, PhD

Research Intern
P. J. Gorman, MDiv

Survey Design
Chris Elisara, PhD

Director of Communications, CHI
Claire Cusick, MA

Research Fellow
Jordan Baucum, MBA

Advisory Board

Contents

List of Figures | xi

List of Abbreviations | xiii

Foreword by Christopher J. Adams | xv

Acknowledgments | xix

1 Who Cares for Clergy? | 1

2 How We Got Here | 16

3 The Making of a Clergy Care Provider | 41

4 We Aren't Reading the Same Things | 62

5 We Aren't Speaking the Same Language | 73

6 What Are We Providing? | 89

7 Following the Money | 102

8 What's Getting in the Way? | 115

9 Conclusion | 125

Appendix A: Methodology | 131

Appendix B: Survey | 138

Bibliography | 155

List of Figures

Figure 1–1: Clergy Care Sectors | 11

Figure 1–2: Geographic Distribution of Providers | 12

Figure 1–3: Participants by Sector | 14

Figure 3–1: Pastoral Experience by Sector | 43

Figure 3–2: Formal and Informal Training by Sector | 50

Figure 3–3: Types of Formal Training | 51

Figure 3–4: Types of Informal Training | 55

Figure 3–5: Comparison of No Training with Both Types of Training | 57

Figure 4–1: Academic Word Cloud | 65

Figure 4–2: Participants' Word Cloud | 65

Figure 4–3: Topics Covered | 66

Figure 4–4: Audiences | 70

Figure 5–1: Sectors and Top Four Well-Being Concepts | 78

Figure 5–2: Sectors and Root Causes | 84

Figure 6–1: Identified Needs | 91

Figure 6–2: Types of Support Provided | 99

Figure 7–1: Total Grants ($) vs. Number of Grants | 104

List of Figures

Figure 7-2: Distribution of Funding across Categories | 105

Figure 7-3: Grant Distribution by State | 106

Figure 7-4: Geographic Scope of Programs and Services | 107

Figure 7-5: Budget for Clergy by Sector | 109

Figure 7-6: Estimated Programmatic Budgets | 110

Figure 7-7: Source of Funding | 111

Figure 7-8: Is the Budget Enough? | 113

Figure A-1: Clergy and their Roles | 133

List of Abbreviations

AACC	American Association of Christian Counselors
AAPC	American Association of Pastoral Counselors
ADME	Association for Doctor of Ministry Education
ALLLM	Association of Leaders in Lifelong Learning in Ministry
AME Zion	African Methodist Episcopal Church Zion
ARC	Association of Related Churches
ATS	Association of Theological Schools
CE	Common Era
COGIC	Church of God in Christ
COVID-19	Coronavirus Disease 2019
CTSD	Continuous Traumatic Stress Disorder
DMin	Doctor of Ministry
ESC	Ecumenical Stewardship Center
GLS	Global Leadership Summit
HBCU	Historically Black Colleges and Universities
IBCC	International Board of Christian Care

List of Abbreviations

ICCI	International Christian Coaching Institute
ICF	International Coaching Federation
MDiv	Master of Divinity
MFI	Ministers Fellowship International
MMBB	Ministers and Missionaries Benefit Board
NAUMF	National Association of United Methodist Foundations
NCC	National Council of Churches
NGO	Nongovernmental Organization
PC(USA)	Presbyterian Church (USA)
SACEM	Society for the Advancement of Continuing Education for Ministry
TMF	Texas Methodist Foundation
WCA	Willow Creek Association

Foreword

AS MY GRANDFATHER LAY in a hospital bed following a heart attack in midlife, he said to my father, "You are not much good to the kingdom of God lying flat on your back." I am a third-generation pastor's kid and have heard this story many times. My grandfather, called to vocational ministry in midlife, had to retire from pastoral ministry prematurely and move from Indiana to Florida for the sake of his health. He later died young of a second heart attack. My grandfather was an amazing pastor. At great sacrifice, he worked several jobs and went to Harvard for his MDiv. He faithfully and fruitfully served as the pastor of several small, what I might call "clergy-killing," congregations in New England. Eventually, he became the senior pastor of a fairly large church in the Midwest. He did it all. He cast vision, preached incredible sermons, led worship with his wonderful tenor voice, provided pastoral care and visitation, led board meetings, mowed the church lawn, ran off church bulletins on the mimeograph machine, and . . . and . . . and . . . . No one was researching clergy stress in those days. There was very little acknowledgment, if any, of the various stressors, many hidden and unrecognized by clergy themselves, or the cumulative impact of clergy stress on the health and well-being of pastors. I often wonder how my own grandfather's path might have been different if he had had the support and resources he needed.

My own father has been in music ministry my whole life, both in the local church and in itinerant concert ministry. As a result of his ministry,

I was in hundreds of pastors' homes all over the U.S., across a large spectrum of denominational families. This was a wonderful exposure to many different ecclesiologies and philosophies of ministry—as well as to many joy-filled clergy who were flourishing in their lives and work. I also was exposed to a lot of common pain—isolation, church conflict, family difficulties, financial struggles, and so many other challenges. I began to realize at an early age that clergy need support. In retrospect, the Lord was shaping a burden in me that would later become the focus of my own vocation. I imagine you might have a similar story if you are reading this resource too.

As a pastor and psychologist, I have had the incredible privilege to be invited into circles of clergy and denominations across mainline, Evangelical (denominational and nondenominational), Catholic, and Eastern Orthodox groups. One of the many incredible gifts of my years in researching, consulting, and providing care for clergy has been to realize that there are many wonderful people doing parallel, amazing work to support clergy in different denominations, academic institutions, and organizations—but they often do not know about the work of one another. I began to wonder: what might be possible if we were to network the networks? Researchers and providers could learn from one another without having to recreate resources that may have already been well-developed. What might happen if researchers and practitioners were in continual conversation, in a virtuous cycle of translational research? How would clergy benefit if resources were vetted with professional criteria and best practices? What if there were a way to find out what research, resources, and relationships currently exist? I believe that this book and the Common Table Collaborative (https://commontable.network/) will move us forward toward a burgeoning professionalism and integration of the field of clergy care.

Many years ago, I had the wonderful opportunity to go to Italy with a friend of mine who is also a pastor. He is Italian-American and had been to Italy several times before—so he knew the best places to visit. Having an interest in archaeology and church history, I marveled at the ruins of ancient Rome in the Forum. I was captivated by the century upon century of historically and culturally significant sites. Even the hotel where we stayed was more than five hundred years old. Then, we went to the Vatican. I was deeply moved by the Colonnade in St. Peter's Square, built to symbolize the arms of the church reaching out to embrace the world. I stood in awe of the sheer scope and majesty of St. Peter's Basilica. I remember experiencing a deep sense that I am a part of a story that is much bigger and much older than I am.

I also vividly remember my favorite room in the Vatican Museum—the map room. The hallway after hallway of sculpture and paintings by the great masters of the ages was incredible, but the map room intrigued me. There, in chronological order, hung maps of the world created by explorers as they discovered more and more of planet Earth. You could see the early, crude, partial outlines of continents in the early maps. Perusing the maps through the centuries, I could see how the picture of the world began to fill out with more and more details, more complete accuracy. Building on the work of their predecessors, later explorers would refine the details as mapmaking and exploring technologies advanced.

Explorers began to have access to one another's maps and realized that, in some cases, they were exploring the same parts of the world. Consequently, by coordinating efforts, they were able to be more strategic in their adventures over time, working together to explore and map out new territory. Of course, eventually, humankind developed the ability to fly, and the maps became even more accurate due to additional perspective from above. Then, we created satellite technology, which gave even greater perspective. We now have GPS capability, so a handheld device can locate us on a map anywhere in the world with pinpoint accuracy. And yet during the centuries of technological development, the coastlines also changed. Sea levels rose. Islands formed and others disappeared. Earthquakes, hurricanes, volcanoes, and other natural disasters changed the landscape. So, the maps had to be redrawn, edited, and kept up-to-date in a continual process of rediscovery and shared knowledge.

What we hope to provide in this book is a bit of an early map of the current state of all of those entities that are investing in caring for clergy. Since we are relatively early explorers in mapping out this territory, some pieces of the map are more accurate than others. Over time we will have a more complete, detailed, and accurate picture of the landscape—even as the landscape of ministry leadership changes. We hope that the picture that begins to emerge for you is one that is based in hope.

After my friend and I had spent time at the Vatican Museum, we went to the catacombs outside of Rome. The catacombs were created by early Christians as a place to bury their loved ones. The Romans cremated everyone because it was more efficient and sanitary. However, Christians wanted to preserve the bodies of their loved ones, due to a deep belief in an embodied faith. We had a passionate, Christian tour guide. She pointed out the Christian symbolism carved into the architecture of the catacombs, such as the Greek letters chi and rho (the symbols for Christ) and the fish symbol that you sometimes see on bumper stickers in our own time. Most powerfully, she pointed out that the early Christians intentionally used the Roman arch within the architecture of the catacombs. The Roman arch had come to symbolize victory. When a Roman emperor conquered yet another territory, an arch was often built in celebration. For example, the Arch of Titus in Rome was built after Jerusalem was conquered in 70 CE. Early Christians took the Roman arch and Christianized it as a reminder of the victory of Jesus Christ over all powers, even as they held worship services among the catacombs in order to avoid persecution. We then went to the Circus Maximus. The Circus Maximus is a giant stadium, much like a modern racetrack, that held up to three hundred thousand people. The palace of the Emperor Nero overlooks the stadium. Historians believe this may have been the place where more Christians were martyred than even the famed Coliseum.

As we stood on a small rise in the middle of the Circus Maximus, contemplating the weight and significance of this location for Christians, we caught a view of the dome of St. Peter's Basilica, a powerful reminder that while the Roman Empire, and other empires, have come and gone, the church of Jesus Christ is still here. There is still an arch of victory over the church, as the most resilient movement in history. And Christian leaders have always had and needed support. Moses had Aaron and Hur to hold up his arms. Jesus had the twelve disciples, Mary and Martha, Mary Magdalene, and others. Paul had Barnabas.

Our deep hope as you read this resource is that you will be inspired to know and take your place in the grand story of those who have been encouragers of God's shepherds down through the centuries. We invite you to join the adventure as we discover, map, and engineer, together, the best research and practices to help clergy and other kinds of ministry leaders flourish.

I would like to thank Dr. Thad Austin and Dr. Katie Comeau at Duke for their friendship and leadership in this endeavor as well as my friends at the Duke Clergy Health Initiative. I would also like to express deep gratitude to Rev. Russ Gunsalus and Dr. David Higle from The Wesleyan Church, whose vision and leadership gave birth to what is now the Common Table Collaborative.

Rev. Christopher J. Adams, PhD

Acknowledgments

From the outset of this project, we have been touched by the ministry of those who care for clergy. Their work makes a tremendous impact, not only in the lives of clergy but also in the congregations and communities those clergy serve. They are the inspiration for this book, and we count many of them as friends. We thank the hundreds of clergy care providers who completed our survey or participated in one of our interviews or focus groups, and all who allowed us the opportunity to visit their ministry in person. We have been moved by your passion, perseverance, and commitment.

This book would not have been possible without the generous support of the Duke Endowment's Rural Church program area and the partnership of the Duke Clergy Health Initiative. Since its inception, the Duke Endowment's commitment to enriching lives and strengthening communities has made a profound difference in the church and its leaders. The Duke Endowment has invested generously in education, research, and evidence-based programs that impact clergy. Specifically, we appreciate the guidance and support of Robb Webb and Kristen Richardson-Frick.

We are deeply grateful for the faculty, staff, and administration of Duke Divinity School who shared their expertise, insight, and perspective with us. Among them, we give thanks for Edgardo Colón-Emeric, David Goatley, Carl Weisner, Rae Jean Proeschold-Bell, David Eagle, Alma Ruiz, Brad Thie, Dave Odom, Alaina Kleinbeck, Randy Maddox, Jan Holton, Farr Curlin, Warren Kinghorn, Brett McCarty, Kelly Ryan, Mark Chaves, as well as our Ormond

Acknowledgments

Center colleagues. We express our sincere gratitude to both our academic and practitioner advisory boards for their insight, wisdom, and encouragement. We are indebted to Paige Marie Burr, Carla Foote, and Alex Fulton for their communications, editing, and artistic design expertise. Thank you to Charlie Collier, George Callihan, and the team at Wipf and Stock who believed in this project and have been wonderful collaborators.

I (Thad) thank my family (Courtney, Chloe, Steve, Barbara, Glenn, Linda, Brittany, Garrett, and Graham) for their love, patience, and forbearance during the research and writing of this manuscript. I also express my gratitude to my co-author, Katie Comeau, who stewarded much of the detailed analysis for this project and has contributed to our findings in countless ways.

I (Katie) thank the many people who participated in our research project. Your care and concern for clergy and the church continues to inspire me. My deepest gratitude to my family, friends, and community who supported and encouraged me during the research and writing.

1

Who Cares for Clergy?

EXODUS 17 DESCRIBES A decisive battle between the Israelites and the Amalekites, a semi-nomadic tribe who occupied the central hills and valleys of the Sinai.[1] As Joshua took command of the Hebrew forces for the first time, Moses ascended a hill overlooking the battlefield. Whenever Moses raised his arms, the Israelites prevailed. Scholars speculate that Moses could have been providing encouragement to the troops, petitioning God in prayer, or offering battle instructions for Joshua's forces.[2] Regardless, his actions had a direct and immediate impact on the war that raged. Weary as the sun set, Moses's arms lowered, and the tide began to turn. In need of support, two of Moses's advisors, Aaron and Hur, upheld his hands, and the Israelites defeated the Amalekites that day.

The efforts of Aaron and Hur did more than uphold Moses. They provided support for the entire community of faith. Like Aaron and Hur, such supporters fill the pages of Scripture. Joseph offered grain to his family. Ruth vowed to remain with Naomi. Nathan confronted King David. Martha served the needs of Jesus. Jesus washed the disciples' feet. Barnabas traveled with Paul. Among a great cloud of other witnesses, these supporters offered compassion, mended wounds, upheld spirits, and served others. Their efforts did not skirt the requirement of individual responsibility and

1. See Gen 36:12–15.

2. Hamilton, *Handbook on the Pentateuch*, 189; Exod 17:8, in Matthews et al., *IVP Bible Background Commentary*.

did not fully eliminate the struggles that others faced. Yet, their actions pointed to the presence and provision of God. Together, they display the interconnected power and beauty of the body of Christ.

Why Does Clergy Care Matter?

While leadership is important for any organization, clergy leadership is critical for religious communities. The support clergy receive (or do not receive) has a direct impact upon their effectiveness and overall well-being. In turn, their well-being impacts the flourishing and sustainability of congregations and communities. Although the quantitative and qualitative data we outline in this book certainly underscore the need for and importance of clergy care, we want to address the importance of such support in the first place. There are plenty of other ongoing needs inside and outside the church that also require attention. So, why does supporting clergy matter?

On one hand, we acknowledge the experiences of clergy do not matter more than the experiences of other professionals like medical doctors, teachers, or first responders. Protestantism has long maintained a "cultural egalitarianism" with regard to religious leaders.[3] Martin Luther included clergy in the priesthood of *all* believers because clergy are no different than any other people created in the image of God. However, there are unique demands and expectations for clergy that warrant consideration. We contend that clergy are not meant to labor alone. Their care matters to God, to the church, and to society as a whole.

God cares about clergy support because God cares about all people. Drawing on the command to "Feed my sheep" (John 21:15–17), Flora Slosson Wuellner notes that if God cares about sheep being fed, then God also cares about shepherds being fed.[4] Just as Jesus's ministry focused on restoring the well-being of individuals as a sign of the coming reign of God, clergy support and well-being display an important sign of God's wholeness manifested within the church.

God calls clergy to care for the mission of the church. Their support and well-being matters to God because of the incarnational nature of ministry. Early church father St. Jerome once said, "There can be no church

---

3. Ferguson et al., *New Dictionary of Theology*, 531. See also Eastwood, *Priesthood of All Believers*; Carroll, "Toward 2000," 294.

4. Wuelleer, *Feed My Shepherds*, 11–12.

community without a leader or team of leaders."[5] Just as the Hebrew Scriptures reveal special provisions for the priests and Levites, Christian clergy have a special role within the church.[6] God's kingdom grows more fully when clergy are healthy and whole, and, by contrast, unhealthy and unsupported clergy hinder the mission of God.

Clergy occupy an important and distinctive role through their ministerial office. The well-being of clergy impacts the church's ability to fulfill its mission. Unhealthy clergy distort and potentially damage the way others see and understand the gospel. Consider the example of pastor Mark Driscoll where the elders of Mars Hill Church asked Driscoll to resign because of his abusive and unhealthy behaviors. Mike Cosper, the host of a podcast covering the aftermath of Driscoll's resignation, said, "Many former Mars Hill members in Seattle were so shattered by their experience they left Christianity altogether."[7] Unhealthy leaders jeopardize ministries and contribute to unstable institutions.[8]

By contrast, healthy clergy contribute to healthy congregations and church systems. Supported leaders carry a greater capacity to encourage morale, endure hardships, and bounce back after setbacks. But what is the witness of an unhealthy clergyperson? The actions of leaders are more important than the messages they preach. When faith-based organizations intended for good are led by clergy who are not well, they hurt people. Consider the impact of the sex abuse scandals that have rocked the Roman Catholic Church or the Southern Baptist Convention.[9]

Unsupported clergy produce real and hidden costs for the church. Real costs include higher insurance premiums, damaged reputations, squandered financial resources, and fewer clergy in ministry. Hidden costs include a decrease in trust, innovation, and creativity. Caring for the well-being of clergy must be a priority, not only to avoid the prospect of bad effects but also to optimize the church's potential to bless the lives of individuals and communities.

5. Quoted in Schillebeeckx, *Ministry*, 1.

6. Consider Mal 3:2–4.

7. Tong and Hagan, "Rise and Fall."

8. Organizations may prosper under the leadership of an unhealthy clergyperson. However, this growth is seldom sustainable, can be unhealthy, and may lead to other issues for the clergyperson, the clergyperson's family, the local community, or the institution.

9. "Roman Catholic Church"; Nadolny, "Tongue Is a Fire"; Shellnutt, "Southern Baptists Refused."

Healthy clergy are better equipped to engage society in good works and contribute to the flourishing of the world. Under the leadership of healthy clergy, laity learn how to love people and how to serve others. Along with other members of the body of Christ, clergy help heal and repair our world. Communities often process tragedy and find moral direction within congregations. For example, many people looked to the church to provide a safe space after 9/11.

Unhealthy clergy affect the church's ability to recruit, train, and retain healthy members and leaders. A participant in our research named Bob said that after his congregation dismissed an unhealthy pastor, his congregation did not trust the pastor that followed. The suspicion and mistrust of the new pastor continued for more than seven years. This sentiment impaired the congregation and constrained the leadership of the new pastor, influencing his perception of the congregation and of ministry overall. The whole body of Christ is affected by the health of its leaders.

Clergy well-being matters to society at large because, as shepherds, clergy model behavior for their congregations and contribute to the well-being of their followers. From small, rural towns to large cities, the local pastor provides leadership that brings people together. They have expansive networks reaching almost every community in North America.[10] They gather more people on a regular basis than any other institutional form.[11] Their actions build or erode trust in institutions. People listen to what they say and follow where they go.

The congregations clergy lead possess incredible resources and contribute to the pro-social behavior of their members.[12] They receive almost a third of all charitable donations made in America and oversee diverse resources including land, buildings, and investment holdings.[13] Along with other similar religious entities, congregations are collectively the most common and numerous form of nonprofit organization in America.[14] Healthy, supported clergy contribute to a robust civil society. Clergy have the ears of the well-connected. They stand up for the uncounted, welcome the poor

10. Chaves et al., *Congregations in 21st Century America*; Chaves, *Congregations in America*.

11. King et al., "National Study."

12. Bekkers and Wiepking, "Who Gives?"; Showers et al., "Charitable Giving Expenditures."

13. Lilly Family School of Philanthropy, *Giving USA 2021*; Austin, *Giving USA Special Report*.

14. Fulton, "26. Religious Organizations," 581.

and strangers, speak at city council meetings, and march in demonstrations. Healthy clergy can build bridges across areas of difference and stitch communities together.

A Brief History of Clergy Care and Support

The care and support available to clergy has long been considered by communities of faith. Within the Judeo-Christian tradition, the care of clergy stretches back at least to the time of Moses and Aaron, the first high priest.[15] As the Jewish people left bondage in Egypt, the Israelites established rules and regulations that governed their shared religious life, including expectations regarding clergy leadership that were codified primarily in the books of Leviticus, Numbers, and Deuteronomy.

In those days, priests and Levites functioned as professional religious leaders, first among local places of worship and then—with the establishment of the monarchy—in a more centralized role at the temple in Jerusalem.[16] Clergy were set apart from the general population and supported by the community.[17] Unlike the twelve tribes of Israel, priests did not own land (Num 18:20, Deut 10:9).[18] As Walter Elwell and Philip Comfort note:

> The absence of land . . . meant that [religious leaders] could not support and feed themselves as could other men and women. Consequently, the law specified that they could be supported for their services by the people as a whole. They were to receive, from worshipers, portions of animals that were brought to the tabernacle, as well as corn, wine, oil, and wool.[19]

As a result, support for religious leaders was centralized. Priests and Levites received food and provisions through the worship, offerings, and sacrifices of the community of faith (Neh 10:37–39). Directly, support included

15. Although there is no formal or direct connection between the Jewish priesthood and Christian clerical practice, comparing these two groups has long been part of a conceptual framework to understand the evolution of religious leaders. See Bradshaw, *Rites of Ordination*, 1.

16. Bradshaw, *Rites of Ordination*, 2–3; Elwell and Comfort, *Tyndale Bible Dictionary*, 1073–74; The distinction between priests and Levites remains until the New Testament. See John 1:19, Luke 10:31–32.

17. Ryken et al., *Dictionary of Biblical Imagery*, 662.

18. At some point, this tradition was abandoned. See Acts 4:36–37. Also, some cities were set aside for Levites (Josh 21; Num 35:1–8).

19. Elwell and Comfort, *Tyndale Bible Dictionary*, 1075.

material income from tithes, offerings, and sacrifices. Indirectly, taxes supported the ministry of the religious leaders and the operations of the temple.[20] Additionally, the ministry of priests and Levites was interconnected.[21] The Levites, who had lower social standing than the priests, received the tithe and gave a portion to the priests.[22] Here we begin to see some of the first evidence of clergy caring for other clergy, a theme that continues until modern times.

Prior to the Babylonian exile, priests received modest provisions primarily offered during the act of worship through the sacrificial system.[23] However, the majority of material income that priests received was from tithes of crops, spices, wine, oil, animals, and dough.[24] Following the exile, the income, allowances, and sociopolitical power of priests and Levites increased substantially.[25] The increase in support for clergy corresponded with an increase in position, power, and prestige of their position within Jewish society.[26] In the absence of a king, the religious leaders became an

20. These included the half-shekel tax and wood offering for the temple's sacrificial system. See Schürer et al., *History of Jewish People*, 271–73.

21. Scholars debate the precise relationship between priests and Levites. See Elwell and Comfort, *Tyndale Bible Dictionary*, 1074.

22. Numbers 18:20; Neh 10:38–40. See also Schürer et al., *History of Jewish People*, 263. The explanation for the differing status between priests and Levites can be found in Ezek 44:10–31.

23. Schürer et al., *History of Jewish People*, 257. Deuteronomy specifies that the Levites and the poor receive provision from sacrificial worship every three years (Deut 14:22–29; 26:12–15; 12:6; 11:17–19). Priests received only a portion of the worshiper's sacrifice. The portion was to be the best of the fields, the firstborn of animals (Num 18:15–18), certain portions of animals (Deut 18:3; Lev 7:30–34), the first fleece from sheep (Deut 18:4), and the first of the dough (Ezek 44:28–30). However, material income was primarily generated through the introduction of the tithe, requiring the Jewish people to give from their first fruits (see Num 18:8–32).

24. Schürer et al., *History of Jewish People*, 262.

25. J. Green and Hurst, "Priest, Priesthood." Also, as influential members of society, priests and some Levites were deported to Babylon where formalized religious practice was forbidden (Jer 29:1). The Persian Empire allowed the Jews to return to their homes. Among those who were permitted to return, more than 4,000 were priests (or part of their families) and 341 were Levites (Ezra 2:36–42). Once at home, they helped restore the temple and resume religious practice.

26. Schürer et al, *History of Jewish People*, 257. Reinstitution of the practices of giving are specified in Neh 10:36–40. Also, the number of religious leaders grew such that they would serve at the temple only for a week at a time, residing at home during the other times and supplementing their income in other ways. Bradshaw, *Rites of Ordination*, 4.

aristocratic class.[27] By the time of Jesus, clergy were given portions of meat from regular offerings.[28] They obtained grain from grain offerings.[29] Bread was given from food offerings,[30] and clergy received material possessions from offerings of consecration and restitution.[31]

Like the religious leaders of the Hebrew Scriptures, Jesus and his disciples received support directly and indirectly. However, their support was not centralized. Instead, small groups of supporters provided for their needs. Jesus and the disciples relied on the direct support of voluntary donations from patrons, notably from both men and women (Luke 8:1–3). These supporters included prominent officials such as Joseph of Arimathea and Nicodemus and those without position or authority, like Mary Magdalene.

Individuals like Zacchaeus (Luke 19) and families like Mary and Martha (Luke 10) offered hospitality by welcoming Jesus and his disciples into their homes and providing meals for them. In the time leading up to and including his death, supporters provided a donkey for Jesus's triumphant entry into Jerusalem (Matt 21), carried his cross (Matt 27), secured a tomb (Mark 15:43–47), and anointed his body for burial (Luke 23:55–56, John 19:38–41). In addition to these direct and indirect forms of external support, Jesus and his disciples may have also participated in what we would now call bivocational work to support their own needs (Mark 6:3).

Through the death and resurrection of Jesus (Heb 9:12, 14, 26; 10:10), the New Testament church ceased the practice of animal sacrifice and thereby abandoned the Hebrew notion of the priesthood.[32] Since that time, the ministry of Jesus—our High Priest (Heb 4:14)—has been the model for Christian ministry.[33] Jesus cared for his disciples by instructing them, calling them away on retreat (Mark 6:30–34), washing their feet (John 13:1–17), praying for them (John 17:9), and commissioning them (Matt 28:18).

---

27. Bradshaw, *Rites of Ordination*, 3–4.

28. These included sin, guilt, burnt, and thank offerings. Only the most sacred of offerings were for priests only. All others could be enjoyed by members of the priest's household. Thank offerings are also referred to as "communion sacrifices."

29. These were offered frequently in conjunction with animal sacrifice. For matters of frequency, see Lev 11–15; Num 19. Elwell and Comfort, *Tyndale Bible Dictionary*, 972.

30. See Lev 24.

31. These include votive offerings (Lev 27; Deut 23:22–24; Matt 15:5; Mark 7:11) and anathema offerings (Lev 27:28; Num 18:14; Ezek 44:29). Examples of offerings of restitution may be found in Num 5:5–8.

32. Davies, "Sacrifice, Offerings, Gifts."

33. Osborne, *Orders and Ministry*, 41–53.

Alluding to the way Hebrew priests and Levites were supported directly through the sacrificial system, the apostle Paul asserts that those "who proclaim the gospel should get their living by the gospel" (1 Cor 9:9–14). Indeed, Paul accepted support from churches (e.g., Phil 4:15–18, 2 Cor 11:8–9) and individuals (e.g., Acts 16:15, 40). However, he was careful to note that while he had a right to be fully supported in his ministry, he did not take advantage of that right (1 Cor 9:14; 2 Cor 11:7). Like Jesus, Paul worked with his hands supporting himself as a tentmaker (Acts 18:3; 1 Cor 4:12; 2 Thess 3:8).

In the book of Ephesians, Paul describes the offices of ministry, which include apostles, prophets, evangelists, pastors, and teachers (4:11). However, there was no uniform expression of religious leadership in the early New Testament house churches.[34] Although the early church had begun to define some ministerial offices (e.g., Acts 6:2–4), a formalization of clericalism (and specifically the notion of "ordination") did not begin until after the year 200 CE when the Christian notion of the "priesthood" developed.[35] At that time, the church established an ecclesiastical structure with an understanding of clergy as set apart from laity through sacred orders.[36]

Early Christian leaders such as Cyprian drew upon the Hebrew Scriptures (e.g., Num 18) to defend the financial support of clergy and argued that religious leaders should not be forced into employment outside of the church.[37] Similarly, the *Didache*—an early Christian treatise on ethics, worship, and church administration—notes that religious leaders are "worthy of support" and calls upon believers to show hospitality to their clerics and to provide for their leaders out of their first fruits (12, 13.1–3).[38] As with Jesus, religious leaders relied on the gifts of laity.

In 325 CE, when Constantine installed Christianity as the official state religion, a seismic shift took place in the relationship between the church and society.[39] This revolutionary political change had implications for the

34. Bradshaw, *Rites of Ordination*, 17, 24.

35. Rearden, "Priesthood, High and Low?," 541; Bradshaw, *Rites of Ordination*, 41.

36. Osborne, *Orders and Ministry*, 42–43. Early Christian theologian and philosopher Clement of Alexandria may have been the first to use the term *clergy*. See Bradshaw, *Rites of Ordination*, 40.

37. Bradshaw, *Rites of Ordination*, 17, 43.

38. Believers, however, are encouraged to be discerning. According to the *Didache*, one of the signs of a false prophet is if they focus exclusively on their need for money (11.10).

39. See Lenski, *Cambridge Companion*.

way that clergy were supported. Clergy were given a status previously afforded to pagan priests. Namely, they were exempt from taxes and free from public service.[40] As T. G. Elliott states:

> There was no sense in having someone become a cleric in order
> to starve while working for people too poor to support him, nor
> in having him spend time at his business in order to pay the tax
> collector if the imperial policy was to have the poor supported by
> the churches.[41]

This period was marked both by centralization of civic power and continued support of local communities. Although some clergy continued to practice other trades in addition to their ministry, other clergy took on full-time Christian service.[42] The government issued financial grants to support clergy, many of whom were on payroll.[43] Most income gained by the church came from voluntary donations and rental income from church owned property. Other support came through gifts of food, textiles, furniture, flowers, and animals. Some clerics received substantial income, although those in rural areas were paid poorly.[44]

By the early Middle Ages, clerical ministry had become a formalized vocation with rites of ordination and an established career path.[45] Although some clergy were educated in secular or religious schools (like Alexandria and Edessa), there is no evidence of formal education, exclusively for clergy, prior to the time of St. Augustine.[46] At that time, the bishop of Hippo established a *monasterium clericorum* in his home for the training of priests. This model was later replicated throughout the Christian world. In 529 CE, the Council of Vaison encouraged local priests also to adopt this practice of opening their homes and training future ministers. Additionally, cathedral schools and monasteries began offering training.

---

40. Rubenstein, *When Jesus Became God*, 71.

41. T. Elliott, "Tax Exemptions Granted," 329.

42. In the eastern Mediterranean, clergy were salaried at rates determined by the bishop. In the western Mediterranean, clergy were compensated by receiving a share of offerings and rental income. Serfass, "Church Finances," 18, 23, 30–32, 61. See also T. Elliott, "Tax Exemptions Granted," 335.

43. Serfass, "Church Finances," 18, 23, 31–32.

44. Serfass, "Church Finances," 1, 6, 7, 33.

45. Bradshaw, *Rites of Ordination*, 17, 133.

46. Viéban, "Ecclesiastical Seminary."

With time, cathedral schools grew into universities that trained the most elite in the disciplines of theology, philosophy, and canon law. However, these courses had little to no emphasis on spiritual formation. Anthony Viéban estimates that fewer than 1 percent of priests during this period benefited from a university education.[47] In fact, it was not until after the Reformation at the Council of Trent in 1545 that formalized requirements for clergy education were set forth by the Roman Catholic Church and required every diocese to have a seminary.[48]

Prior to the Protestant Reformation, clergy care was simpler. The institutional church attended to the care of clergy, and most priests did not marry. With the Reformation, the structure of the church and the family units of clergy changed dramatically. Protestant churches decentralized the institutional church, and many clergy married and started families. The support of clergy now included other family members.

During this period of tremendous ecclesiastical change, the laity assumed more direct responsibility for the care of clergy. As church historian Esther Chung-Kim notes:

> Since Protestants had allowed and even encouraged clergy to marry, the families of married clergy needed additional support. Mindful of their wives' and children's vulnerability, married clergy emphasized their concern for widows and orphans. . . . The needs of the poor were not a distant theoretical problem, but rather an imminent danger for educated ministers who found themselves struggling to support themselves and their families. As this situation became a persistent problem, [Johannes] Bugenhagen would advocate more strenuously in his later church orders for the provision of pastors and preachers struggling with inadequate resources.[49]

This moment in history marks a shift in how the church regarded its responsibility to care for clergy. Since that time, we have seen the church continue to ebb and flow in how it views its responsibility for clergy support, ultimately impacting the allocation of resources in the church and programs offered for clergy.

47. Viéban, "Ecclesiastical Seminary."
48. Kirsch, "Council of Trent"; Cross and Livingstone, "Seminary."
49. Chung-Kim, *Economics of Faith*, 61.

How We Examined the Network of Clergy Care Providers

Despite the importance of clergy to God, the church, and to society, there has never before been a systematic review of the multi-sector support network upon which clergy rely. This book examines the organizations and individuals who support clergy on a daily basis. This broad system of supporters, whom we will refer to as "clergy care providers," consists of five sectors: (1) denominations, networks, and associations; (2) funders and granting organizations; (3) pension, benefit, and insurance organizations; (4) frontline providers (counselors, coaches, therapists, spiritual directors, licensed clinical social workers, and retreat center hosts); and (5) continuing education institutions. We will expand on each of these sectors in chapter 2.

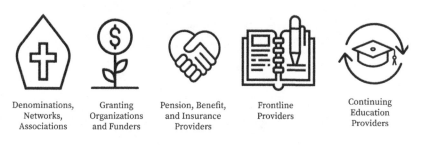

Denominations, Networks, Associations	Granting Organizations and Funders	Pension, Benefit, and Insurance Providers	Frontline Providers	Continuing Education Providers

Figure 1–1: Clergy Care Sectors

While we recognize that some of the most meaningful support that clergy receive occurs at the local level, we chose to examine the institutions and individuals caring for clergy in large numbers because collectively they have the ability to systemically impact pastors across North America.

Our efforts began with a survey of 740 senior-level individuals from within the five sector networks identified above who provide support to clergy. Our survey garnered a 47 percent response rate. Beyond surveying these individuals, we also got to know many of them. We conducted in-depth interviews and focus groups with these providers and made site visits to where they conduct their ministry.

The following map (figure 1–2) reveals where our participants are located.[50] We believe our database serves as the most comprehensive and up-to-date directory of senior-level clergy care providers in North America.

50. Our database provides us with the most comprehensive count of clergy care organizations that exists. The database was constructed by incorporating various lists that organizations and networks maintain of their providers and also by snowball sampling.

The following map was color coded to indicate the completion rate from our survey. Our participants provide care across the United States and Canada.

Completed   Uncompleted

Figure 1–2: Geographic Distribution of Providers

In a typical year, the total number of clergy served by our participants approaches 222,000.[51] While there is likely overlap from the same clergy accessing services from multiple providers, the substantial size of the total clergy population served indicates that our participants likely care for a majority of Protestant clergy in the United States and parts of Canada. Even by conservative estimates, the providers we sampled collectively support more than half of the Protestant clergy in America.[52]

51. We acknowledge that the global pandemic may have had a dramatic impact on the care our participants provide, either increasing or decreasing their normal programs or services. Therefore, we asked our participants to specify the total number of clergy served pre-COVID to ensure that we represented a more normal time. On average, organizations represented in our study cared for 82 clergy pre-COVID.

52. As of 2019, the United States Census Bureau estimates that there are 348,811 clergy in America. According to the National Study of Religious Leaders, Protestant clergy represent 60 percent of this total (209,287 clergy). Collectively, our providers support 221,980. We believe that there is likely substantial overlap in the clergy served by our participants. Assuming a 50 percent overlap, however, our participants support half

Additionally, our participants represent a variety of organizations across the field of clergy caregiving. Some participants serve clients from many professions while others only care for clergy. We have large, complex multi-million-dollar organizations in our sample as well as small practices of one or two people. Some participants provide support for clergy of varying denominational backgrounds and theological traditions while others serve only a single denomination or theological tradition.

Despite this variation, 100 percent of our participants care for clergy in some capacity.[53] Therefore, we are confident that our participants have knowledge and experience supporting and meeting the needs of clergy. We have further evidence of their authority to speak on behalf of their ministries based on the positions they occupy as senior leaders of their organizations. We asked each participant to share their job title within their organization. The most common job titles are leadership roles such as executive, director, and president.[54]

Our participants come from varying theological traditions, divided almost equally between mainline Protestant and evangelical/conservative Protestant traditions.[55] They represent a wide range of theological traditions, denominational polities, and contexts. Although not all sectors contain the same number of organizations,[56] the proportion of organizations is representative of the proportions in the field of clergy caregiving (figure 1–3). The pension, benefit, and insurance sector, while less than 10 percent of our sample overall, includes representation from half of

---

of Protestant clergy in America. For reference, see United States Census Bureau, "American Community Survey"; National Congregations Study, "National Survey of Religious Leaders."

53. Ninety-one percent provide care directly (they personally interact with and oversee the care of clergy), and 9 percent of our participants care for clergy indirectly (work with others who care for clergy or conduct research). At the beginning of our survey, we asked participants if they are directly responsible for overseeing or providing programs or services for clergy. If they are not directly responsible, we then ask if they are indirectly responsible for caring for clergy. Participants were not able to continue the survey if they did not either directly or indirectly care for clergy.

54. A number of academics who serve resource centers and continuing education institutions are also included.

55. There are a few Roman Catholics and Orthodox in our sample. We did not intentionally reach out to them, but several took the survey as representatives of their organization.

56. For instance, there are more frontline provider organizations in North America than pension, benefit, and insurance organizations in North America.

the organizations providing insurance services to Protestant clergy in the United States and Canada.[57]

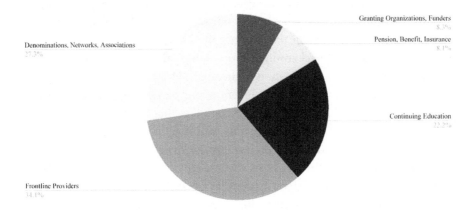

Granting Organizations, Funders
8.3%

Pension, Benefit, Insurance
8.1%

Denominations, Networks, Associations
27.3%

Continuing Education
22.2%

Frontline Providers
34.1%

Figure 1–3: Participants by Sector

In addition to our survey, we conducted more than forty interviews, held nine focus groups, and made six site visits to ministry locations in four regions of the United States. We utilized these interviews, focus groups, and site visits to better understand the key themes that emerged from our survey responses. This led us to interviewing clergy care providers in the very beginning stages of providing care as well as those who had been in their role for decades. The themes that emerged from our survey also guided us to interview leaders who provide care for bivocational clergy, women clergy, and clergy of color.

Because our survey primarily asked about organization-level data, it did not ask for demographic information from our participants. Therefore, we do not know the race, ethnicity, or gender of our participants. However, we intentionally reached out to those who primarily care for clergy of color, those who represent Black Protestant denominations, and those who serve women clergy. We hosted focus groups to specifically learn from and discuss the unique concerns associated with these often-underrepresented populations.

57. Our sample has representation from half of the members of the Church Benefits Association and organizations that are not associated with the Church Benefits Association but provide insurance and benefits services for clergy.

Conclusion

In the pages that follow, we will detail the findings of the first comprehensive study of Protestant clergy care providers and the life-changing work they do. These individuals and organizations offer programs and services that provide counsel, direction, funding, hospitality, education, and benefits upon which clergy rely. Many serve selflessly and generously.

Unfortunately, our findings uncover significant challenges that restrict the ability of providers to offer full and appropriate support. We find a disconnected network of providers with deep silos and little coordination. The network has little to no common standards, goals, training, language, or measures to evaluate the care provided. There is little empirical grounding in providers' resources as well as substantive gaps between their sources and academic research. We find significant differences in the care that underserved populations of clergy receive compared to the majority population. Furthermore, most of our participants were clergy themselves. Some providers still carry open wounds from their own time in local church ministry and need healing and support themselves.

This book tells the story of clergy care providers and the challenging, yet important and necessary work they do to advance God's kingdom. It also tells the story of a disconnected network. With concerted effort, prayer, resources, and willingness among diverse stakeholders to collaborate, we can address and potentially overcome some of the challenges the network faces. If you are one of these providers, our hope is that this book will enlighten and encourage you in the care you provide. If you are a clergyperson, we hope that this resource will be of help as you navigate the complex and often disconnected support network available to you. Finally, if you are a layperson, we hope this book will give you fresh insight into the needs of clergy and prompt you to consider how you might be uniquely positioned to care for them in your local congregation.

2

How We Got Here

ON JANUARY 12, 2010, a 7.0 magnitude earthquake shook the Caribbean island nation of Haiti, leaving more than 200,000 people dead, 300,000 injured, and 1.5 million homeless.[1] After the earthquake, an immediate need for aid triggered individuals and organizations from around the world to channel more than $9 billion dollars towards relief.[2] Swiss Solidarity, a humanitarian foundation, invested over 62 million francs for the effort and partnered with nongovernmental organizations (NGOs) to rebuild houses, restore clean drinking water, and provide for other basic needs.[3] CARE International, Oxfam, the Red Cross, and Food for the Poor are among others who donated money, supplies, and personnel towards providing immediate relief. Despite this abundance of financial resources and support from a wide variety of NGOs, recovery efforts stalled.

These organizations lacked shared goals, a common understanding of root problems, and an ability to communicate with each other effectively. News outlets widely reported that this lack of coordination had a detrimental impact on recovery efforts, led to an inefficient use of funds, and delayed crucial services. For example, the Red Cross raised $500 million to help Haitians recover from the earthquake. Despite the claim that they used

1. United Nations, "Rebuilding Haiti."
2. Ramachandran and Walz, "Haiti's Earthquake."
3. Juillard et al., "Haiti + 10 Impact Evaluation."

these funds to build enough housing for over 130,000 Haitians, in reality, the Red Cross had built only six permanent homes by 2015.[4]

Earthquakes are devastating natural disasters, but the 2010 Haiti earthquake became a catastrophe due to systemic lack of coordination and misunderstanding of needs by outside NGOs providing assistance.[5] Today, while much of the rubble from the 2010 earthquake has been cleared, general conditions remain the same, if not worse, than they had been shortly after the earthquake. Before the COVID-19 pandemic, Haiti's medical system was already on the verge of collapse.[6] Despite all the resources and attention the country had received just a few years before, there was little long-term benefit due to a failure of coordination among NGOs and a failure of imagination for what Haiti could become after the earthquake.

Our Crisis: Many Clergy Need Support[7]

The church has been dealing with its own crisis. Researchers and commentators of American religion have consistently described pastoral ministry as intense and overwhelming. According to a 2015 Lifeway study of evangelical pastors, 54 percent of pastors agreed their role was "frequently overwhelming" and 48 percent agreed that "the demands of ministry are more than they can handle."[8] In 2021, these numbers increased to 63 percent and 50 percent respectively, showing that pastors face increasing challenges in ministry.[9] During the COVID-19 pandemic, their workload intensified. Compared to the pre-COVID era, some pastors have described this change as "unprecedented."[10] Consequently, the work and complexity of clergy care providers has also increased during this time.

The pandemic amplified the problem of clergy burnout for many pastors. The skills required for effective ministry today differ compared to what

---

4. J. Elliott and Sullivan, "How Red Cross Built."

5. Sael et al., "Decade after the Earthquake."

6. Médecins Sans Frontières, "Ten Years."

7. The outlook for clergy is not totally bleak. While clergy, on average, fare worse than the general population in measures of physical and mental/emotional health, many clergy do experience fulfilling ministries and good health.

8. L. Green, "Despite Stresses."

9. Lifeway Research, "Study of Pastor Attrition."

10. Topper, "Too Many Pastors Are Falling."

they were just a few years ago.[11] Clergy who previously may have needed minimal or no training in technology had to quickly transition to offering online worship services, Bible studies, and small groups.[12] Additionally, the move to online services exacerbated instances of loneliness and isolation among clergy.

Church leaders navigated complex guidelines about meeting and mask-wearing, requiring the knowledge and ability to speak about controversial public health and public policy mandates.[13] These decisions became politicized, often alienating a significant portion of their congregations.[14] Caught in the middle, pastors faced increased criticism. In many cases, clergy had to simultaneously navigate vaccination efforts and requests for religious exemptions from COVID-19 vaccines.[15]

Political and racial tensions also increased during the pandemic. Some congregations applied pressure on their clergy to resign for being "divisive" after attempting to address social and political issues, such as preaching against Christian nationalism or warning about the spread of misinformation and conspiracy theories.[16] Jonathan Davis compares the treatment some clergy receive to a kind of abusive domestic relationship that includes "telling a partner they never do anything right, showing unhealthy jealousy for someone's time, and controlling the finances of another."[17] To the clergy with whom Davis has spoken, these characteristics are familiar. Oftentimes, when clergy leave ministry, it is the result of a "death by a thousand paper cuts" caused by various forms of abuse from their congregants. Additionally, Davis and Melissa Florer-Bixler describe diseases of racism and sexism present in ministry contexts, even among those who claim they are loving and progressive.[18]

Under increased pressure, rates of depression and suicide have increased among clergy in the twenty-first century.[19] Clergy describe feeling isolated and experiencing difficulty making true friendships with

---

11. Gorny, "Christ the King Pastor."

12. Anderson, "Closed Doors, Virtual Services"; Gorny, "Christ the King Pastor."

13. Vanderweele and Case, "Empty Pews."

14. Ankel, "Pastors Are Leaving."

15. Khurana, "Religious Leaders Caught."

16. Bumgardner, "They Spoke Out."

17. Davis, "If You Are."

18. Florer-Bixler, "Why Pastors Are Joining."

19. Moore, "Ed Moore."

congregants and lay leaders.[20] Within the last decade, scholars find instances of depressive symptoms among clergy to be nearly twice the rate found in the general population.[21] This disparity between the general population and clergy is slightly greater for clergymen than for women clergy because more women in general have symptoms of depression.

Despite this shocking statistic, clergy generally avoid seeking help for depression out of fear for professional consequences and because of the stigma around mental health in some Christian contexts.[22] The topic of mental health within Christian churches has been discussed for a number of years. Generally, stigma exists around Christians seeking help with mental health related issues, especially among pastors in evangelical churches.[23] Pastors might also fail to seek help from counselors or therapists because they lack the financial ability to do so. As Tracy Dawson suggests, pastors "feel they lack compassionate, supportive resources to turn to even as they approach the breaking point."[24]

In January 2021, a study by the Barna Group gained national attention revealing that 29 percent of pastors seriously considered quitting full-time ministry in the previous year. When repeated in October 2021, their estimate increased to 38 percent.[25] Although a study by Lifeway Research challenges these findings, a report by the Hartford Institute for Religion Research found similar results to the Barna study.[26] The exact reasons for pastors leaving churches are complex. Some pastors leave because of abusive church situations or poor congregational support. Others feel that they are no longer up to the task of leading their church or that the ministry they are doing no longer aligns with their career and calling.[27] David Kinnaman, who contributed to the Barna study, explains this increased departure due to the longevity of the pandemic, intense congregational divisions, and

20. Morrison, "Wheaton Summit."

21. Hybels et al., "Persistent Depressive Symptoms."

22. Moore, "Ed Moore"; Morrison, "Wheaton Summit."

23. Morrison, "Wheaton Summit."

24. Dawson, "Whose Problem."

25. Barna Group, "38% of U.S. Pastors." Other research published by Lifeway contests some of these findings.

26. Lifeway Research, "Study of Pastor Attrition"; Hartford Institute for Religion Research, "Navigating the Pandemic"; Barna Group, "38% of U.S. Pastors."

27. Stephens-Reed, "Coming Tidal Wave"; Jonathan Davis, "If You Are"; Gorny, "Christ the King Pastor."

financial strain leading to pastors becoming unhealthier and "experiencing significant burnout."[28]

The significant rise in clergy seriously considering quitting full-time ministry comes as expectations of ministers have increased. Clergy struggle with these growing demands, as Kevin Carson describes, because the pastor "bears the burden of the church as an organism, a body, and in some sense a business."[29] Coinciding with an expanding job description, many clergy face declining or inadequate resources to support their congregation's operations and ministry. Since 2007, the Pew Research Center reports membership declines across all denominations and significant decreases in the percentage of Americans who identify as Christian.[30] Exacerbating this trend, not every member may return to in-person worship following the COVID-19 pandemic.[31] In March 2022, approximately one-third of congregants continued to attend online, although reports indicate that 90 percent of congregations have resumed in-person gatherings.[32] Dwindling attendance can further depress pastoral morale.

The increasing severity of need within the church is alarming. Considered another way, it invites us to examine how clergy are currently supported through the challenges they face in ministry and what can be done better. Husband and wife Dr. Richard and Mrs. Donna Dockins have collaborated on several clergy care initiatives. They recognize the urgency of this invitation and are acting on it by investing in the advancement of the current network of clergy care providers, as well as in our understanding of it. Professionally, Dr. Dockins works as a physician and occupational health expert who has spent more than twenty-five years overseeing the global workforce of a Fortune 100 company. He names what we are seeing with clergy today an "occupational crisis." However, the Dockinses have found little solid empirical evidence to understand clergy well-being or the field of those who provide care for clergy. When asked why they have chosen to support initiatives to better understand and address the needs of clergy, Dr. Dockins responded, "If this type of crisis were happening in any other profession, something would be done about it."[33]

28. Barna Group, "38% of U.S. Pastors."
29. Carson, "When Pastor Commits Suicide."
30. Smith, "About Three-in-Ten U.S. Adults."
31. Anderson, "Closed Doors, Virtual Services."
32. Nortey, "More Houses of Worship."
33. Richard and Donna Dockins, interview with authors, 2022.

Our NGOs: The Network of Clergy Care

In action, the five-sector network of clergy care providers on which this book focuses resembles the network of NGOs that entered Haiti after the earthquake. When the earthquake hit, a network of separate, already established individuals and organizations, each with their own complex histories, values, and priorities descended on Haiti to provide support. The same is true for clergy care providers. Clergy care providers comprise a network of individuals and organizations, which we have categorized into sectors, each informed by different historical precedents, shaped by different experiences, and with differing understandings of clergy needs. Each sector offers unique, valuable services and a common desire to support clergy through the difficult challenges outlined above, but, just like the NGOs in Haiti, often without coordination.

In the pages that follow, we will describe each designated sector of clergy care and provide an overview of their respective histories that have shaped where they are today, especially within the context of the United States. This will lay the foundation for conceptualizing in later chapters the deeper implications of a disconnected network attempting to address clergy's needs: communication barriers, different goals and definitions for success, and divergent understandings of root causes.

Denominations, Networks, and Associations

The "denominations, networks, and associations" sector includes individuals and organizations who support clergy as part of denominational, non-denominational, and parachurch entities. For example, the Evangelical Free Church of America and the Wesleyan Church both have national offices dedicated to the care of their pastors. Other denominational bodies have regional representatives who fulfill such roles. Another example is the Center for Well-Being, established by the Holston Conference of the United Methodist Church, offering professional counseling services to clergy and their families. "Networks and associations" refer to parachurch organizations that connect based on similar values and purpose. Leadership Network and Ministers Fellowship International (MFI) fall into this category.

In their most basic function, denominations are religious associations made up of like-minded individuals who are organized around theology, church polity, and structure. Historically, denominational bodies have been the conduit through which the care of Protestant clergy has formalized. This is especially true in the establishment of denominational seminaries and divinity schools; denominational pension, benefit, and insurance organizations; and to a lesser degree denominational foundations. Outside of these denominationally affiliated organizations, however, the function and orientation of denominations toward clergy has been much more like a "human resources" department that credentials, ordains, and at times disciplines clergy rather than a resource exclusively focused on the care of clergy.

In colonial America, clergy were supported by the church, which in most cases was also part of the state. Following the American Revolution and with the guarantee of free speech, religious expression, and voluntary association, the Constitution supported the development of a wide variety of denominational bodies in America.[34] As these entities grew, new structures needed to be formed for the care and support of clergy.

A 2020 Gallup survey found that fewer than half of U.S. adults claimed membership in any religious institution.[35] Although historically Black Protestant churches have kept stable membership numbers, the cultural trend of disaffiliation from religious institutions and denominations has gained attention within the public media.[36] As many Christian denominations face decline, tighter budgets, and downsizing, clergy care sometimes takes a backseat to other programs and initiatives. In the course of our research, we met a mainline denominational representative whose position focused on clergy support. In the last nine months, his position was eliminated due to budget cuts. He is now serving in a local congregation as a pastor.

In place of and in addition to denominational structures, both networks and professional associations that support pastors have emerged. These organizations provide resources across denominations including those without a denominational affiliation. In the late 1980s and early 1990s groups like MFI, Leadership Network, the Willow Creek Association (WCA), and its Global Leadership Summit (GLS) formed to provide training, resources, and accountability for pastoral leaders, especially within independent churches not served by denominational bodies.[37] The leader of the WCA and GLS, Bill Hybels, resigned in 2019 after credible allegations

34. McConnell, "Reclaiming Secular and Religious."

35. Jones, "U.S. Church Membership Falls."

36. Pew Research Center, "America's Changing Religious Landscape."

37. See https://mfileader.org/about/; https://leadnet.org/about/; Zavada, "Willow Creek Association."

of sexual misconduct were brought against him.[38] Since that time, the GLS lost revenue and, amplified by the pandemic, has seen varying attendance patterns.[39]

Opportunities also emerged for pastors within nondenominational contexts through networks such as the Association of Related Churches (ARC), which was founded in 2000.[40] Organizations like this provide many of the benefits of belonging to a denominational structure. Additionally, professional associations, like the CareGivers Forum, work to bring together clergy care providers, including retreat center hosts, Christian counselors and coaches, and continuing educators to name a few.[41] In 2019, Duke Divinity School's Ormond Center, the Wesleyan Church, and Azusa Pacific University created the Common Table Collaborative to bring together researchers and practitioners interested in clergy and congregational well-being.[42]

Granting Organizations and Funders

The "granting organizations and funders" sector includes several types of organizations that provide funding for clergy support. These organizations primarily include private and denominational foundations. While foundations do not account for a large portion of the overall donations received by religion broadly,[43] foundations can deploy resources strategically at critical moments or in important areas, such as clergy care.[44]

Funders

Most major foundations, including Ford, Rockefeller, Pew, Lilly, and Duke have launched initiatives supporting the church and clergy in particular. However, the commitment to religious causes has become more "unusual"

38. Miller, "Misconduct Allegations Are Credible."

39. K. Roberts, "Global Leadership Network."

40. See https://www.arcchurches.com/about/.

41. CareGivers Forum, "Directory of Ministries." CareGivers Forum began in 1989 to provide a platform for communication and the establishment of a single database for clergy in need. See CareGivers Forum, "History of CareGivers Forum."

42. See https://commontable.network.

43. Lilly Family School of Philanthropy, *Giving USA 2021*.

44. Lindsay and Wuthnow, "Financing Faith," 87.

with time.[45] Take, for instance, the case of J. D. Rockefeller. Motivated by his Baptist faith and a belief that clergy leadership is essential for the church, Rockefeller supported theological institutions and seminarians in need.[46] In the decade leading up to the twentieth century, Rockefeller collectively gave more than half a million dollars to more than thirty Baptist educational institutions, including Black seminaries.[47] Today, the Rockefeller Foundation's work supporting clergy has been eclipsed by other worthwhile efforts promoting health and human flourishing throughout the world.[48]

Other foundations such as the Duke Endowment and Lilly Endowment have maintained their founders' commitments to religious causes and clergy in particular. In the indenture establishing the Duke Endowment, James B. Duke explicitly called for "the care and maintenance of needy and deserving superannuated [Methodist] preachers" and their families.[49] A regional funder, the Duke Endowment's Rural Church program area supports the care of United Methodist clergy in North Carolina.[50] They have supported conferences and continuing education programs for rural pastors; retreats for Black, Asian American, Latinx, and Native American clergy; and research to understand the health and well-being of clergy. In 2008, the Duke Endowment began funding research by Duke Divinity School's Clergy Health Initiative to better understand and improve the well-being of United Methodist clergy in North Carolina.

Similarly, the Lilly Endowment maintains a religion division to "strengthen programs that help congregations adapt and thrive in changing contexts."[51] Motivated by a belief that effective leadership matters for the vitality of congregations,[52] the Lilly Endowment has funded theological and continuing education, sabbatical programs, and cohort experiences enhancing clergy leadership.[53] This focus upon clergy leaders stems from

---

45. Madison, *Eli Lilly*, 209. See also Jungclaus, "Secularizing Philanthropy," 380.

46. Seim, "Rockefeller Philanthropy."

47. Rose and Stapleton, "Toward a 'Universal Heritage.'"

48. See https://www.rockefellerfoundation.org/about-us/.

49. Duke, "Indenture of Trust."

50. Duke Endowment, "Rural Church."

51. Lilly Endowment, "Our Work."

52. Lilly Endowment, "Grant Guidelines and Procedures."

53. For instance, see Cebula, "Thriving in Ministry Grants."

Eli Lilly's commitment to leadership, the church, character development, and desire to make "religion a greater force through his philanthropy."[54]

A range of other funders have also supported clergy. As part of their larger efforts to promote a more "socially conscious" philanthropy in the 1960s, the Ford Foundation funded a training program for Black urban clergy during the civil rights movement.[55] The Murdock Charitable Trust, a regional funder focused exclusively on the Pacific Northwest, has sponsored initiatives on leadership, calling, and mentoring.[56] The McClellan Foundation has sponsored programs geared toward leadership development and generosity.[57] The H. E. Butt Foundation launched a resource center focused on mental health and wellness in and among congregations in the greater San Antonio, Texas, area.[58]

Granting Organizations

For the purpose of our research, "granting organizations" primarily refers to denominational foundations. Typically, these entities provide financial services for denominations and congregations. They manage investment holdings such as congregational endowments and donor advised funds, issue building loans, and offer planned giving programs. In addition to these services, some also offer programming for clergy and congregations. Although some denominational foundations like the Presbyterian Church (USA) [PC(USA)] trace their origins to the nineteenth century, most major denominational foundations were established in the twentieth century. We find that many denominations have a single centralized foundation. Examples of these include the Episcopal Church Foundation, the PC(USA) Foundation, or the Christian Church Foundation.[59] Others, notably among the United Methodist tradition, have independent foundations that are based at the regional level.[60]

---

54. Madison, *Eli Lilly*, 226. See also 204, 209.

55. Lissner, "Ford Aid Is Given."

56. M. J. Murdock Charitable Trust, "Leadership Now."

57. See https://maclellan.net/about.

58. H. E. Butt Foundation, "Job Description."

59. See https://www.ecf.org/about; https://www.presbyterianfoundation.org/about-us/; https://www.christianchurchfoundation.org/about-intro.

60. See http://naumf.org/.

We find that the orientation toward the support of clergy varies greatly among denominational foundations. For some denominational foundations, leadership development and clergy support are a core part of the foundation's mission. For others, their focus is strictly on financial services, leaving the "care" of clergy to other denominational entities, such as denominational pension and benefit boards.

The largest United Methodist Foundation in the United States, the Texas Methodist Foundation (TMF), was founded to provide financial services and promote Christian stewardship in the church. In the 1990s, TMF began to understand a broader mission. As their history narrates, "We began thinking differently about ourselves—not so much as a financial services provider, but as a ministry that offers financial services. We asked ourselves what more we could do to respond to the emerging needs of the church."[61] Since that time, TMF has invested in initiatives to support innovation, courageous leadership, and resources supporting pastoral transitions, to name a few. They host conferences for clergy, establish learning communities, and produce podcasts. Beyond simply managing endowments or issuing loans, TMF understands its ministry as supporting the church and its leaders.

As we will discuss later in more detail, the results of our research show that this sector cares about the financial well-being of clergy. Many denominational foundations issue grants to address the economic considerations of clergy. The most common types of support we see with denominational foundations are through financial stewardship programs, clergy debt reduction programs, sessions with a financial planner, and retirement seminars. Other denominational foundations have programs to provide educational scholarships for clergy, host preaching cohorts or clergy retreats, and administer parental leave programs. Some of these initiatives focus on the early career clergy or those nearing retirement.

We also find that denominational foundations are primarily associated with majority White denominations. In the course of our research, we were unable to identify any active denominational foundations associated with major Black Protestant denominations.[62] We find that Black Protestant denominations are more likely to collect grant opportunities that are

---

61. Texas Methodist Foundation, "Timeline."

62. Our research revealed evidence of an inactive foundation that was associated with a Black Protestant denomination. However, officials from this denominational body confirmed it is no longer active.

available from other entities. For instance, the Church of God in Christ (COGIC) collated a number of grants associated with COVID-19 relief for Black clergy and their congregations.[63] Also, there have been intentional efforts to train and connect Black clergy with major foundations.[64]

The Ecumenical Stewardship Center (ESC) once served as the professional association for many denominational foundations.[65] Founded by the United Stewardship Council of the Christian Church in the United States and Canada and the National Council of the Churches of Christ in the USA in the early twentieth century, ESC spun off as a separate organization to promote Christian stewardship in 1980. Over time, representation in ESC included more than twenty denominations and stewardship organizations in North America. In light of growing budgetary concerns heightened by the global pandemic, ESC closed in 2021, transferring its assets to the Lake Institute on Faith and Giving.[66] Despite the closure, some denominational foundation officials have continued to meet in informal ways. Additionally, because it has regional foundations, the United Methodist Church has maintained a professional association for its members, called the National Association of United Methodist Foundations (NAUMF).[67]

Pension, Benefit, and Insurance Organizations

The "pension, benefit, and insurance" sector includes a variety of organizations that provide pension, benefit, or insurance services for clergy. These organizations offer plans that provide health care insurance and retirement programs. Many of these organizations are denominationally affiliated, but some operate as nonprofit or for-profit organizations, primarily serving nondenominational clergy.

The beginnings of pensions, benefits, and insurance in Protestant churches in America came with the recognition of the need to take care of "worn-out preachers" as well as widows and children.[68] For instance, in the eighteenth century, the Presbyterian Church established a Fund for Pious

63. COGIC Urban Initiatives, "Grant Opportunities."

64. James Davis, "Black Clergy."

65. See https://web.archive.org/web/20201127024242/https://stewardshipresources.org/about/.

66. Lilly Family School of Philanthropy, "Lake Institute."

67. See http://naumf.org/.

68. Faulkner, *Methodists*, 101–2.

Uses that provided financial assistance to the family members of clergy, and the Methodist church established societies to provide benefits for disabled pastors who were unable to support their families.[69] This type of provision was also present within predominantly African American denominations as well. In 1839, the New York Conference of the African Methodist Episcopal Church Zion (AME Zion) established a fund supported and administered by ministers. Clergy each contributed a dollar each year to a common pool, which was available for clergy of congregations who failed to provide adequate "means to support their families."[70] Before the Civil War, when slavery was still practiced in parts of America, this fund provided mutual aid to clergy. In 1884, the AME Zion expanded this model, establishing the Preacher's Aid and Endowment Society.[71]

The modern practice of retirement gained momentum in America at the beginning of the twentieth century. Following Andrew Carnegie's establishment of a retirement fund for educators in 1905,[72] a number of denominational bodies set up pension funds for clergy in the early twentieth century. In 1908, the Methodist Episcopal Church set up what is now known as Wespath Benefits and Investments for aging clergy.[73] In 1911, the National Baptist Convention created an organization "to promote interest in the maintenance of the ministry," which eventually became MMBB (the Ministers and Missionaries Benefit Board).[74] The Christian Methodist Episcopal Church established the General Board of Personnel Services in 1918,[75] and in 1919, the Disciples of Christ Board of Ministerial Relief adopted a ministerial pension system for clergy, allocating $500 per year to eligible ministers.[76]

69. Faulkner, *Methodists*, 101–2. The Disciples of Christ set up a Board of Ministerial Relief in 1895 and, similar to the early colonial preachers' funds, it began by offering support to a pastor's widow and children. Pension Fund of the Christian Church, "History."

70. Bradley, *History of A. M. E. Zion*, 169.

71. Bradley, *History of A. M. E. Zion*, 170.

72. Carnegie Corporation of New York, "Origins of Carnegie Foundation."

73. Wespath Benefits and Investments, "Caring for Those Who Serve."

74. Ministers and Missionaries Benefit Board, "Timeline."

75. Christian Methodist Episcopal Church General Board of Personnel Services, "General Board."

76. Pension Fund of the Christian Church, "History." In 1928, the board was renamed the Pension Fund of the Disciples of Christ and is now known as the Pension Fund of the Christian Church, which retains the same responsibilities of managing ministerial relief and pensions.

Along with these and other denominational efforts, a professional association among these denominational bodies emerged, as in 1915 the newly-formed Church Benefits Association held its first meeting.[77] Over time, this professional association has grown to offer annual meetings and resources for its member organizations. Today, denominational pension, benefit, and insurance programs collectively oversee tens of billions of dollars in assets. For instance, in 2020, Wespath Benefits and Investments, which is associated with the United Methodist Church, reported managing over $28 billion in assets.[78] As of 2020, the Disciples of Christ Pension Fund manages $3.3 billion in assets, has paid out more than $2 billion in pension benefits over its history, and has provided tens of millions of dollars for ministerial relief.[79] The allocation of resources, however, demonstrates vast inequalities, with financial holdings concentrated within majority populations. For comparison, the AME Church pension plan only had a value of $126 million.[80]

The story of these pension and benefits programs is not just one of easily managing and accumulating assets over a century or more. Longer life spans pose a challenge to pension and health benefits, increasing costs and needs of clergy, even as the number of "supporters" or church members decreases.[81] Compounding this problem further is the general trend of lowering the retirement age for receiving church pensions. Lowering the retirement age for eligibility for pension funds to 65 was viewed as posing a significant challenge to the effectiveness of the ministries and pension system of the Church Pension Fund, the administrator of pension funds for The Episcopal Church, as early as 1956.[82]

Outside of denominational pension and benefit programs, a number of for-profit insurers offer their services to the church and clergy in particular. Among these are Brotherhood Mutual and Church Mutual. Brotherhood

---

77. See https://www.churchbenefitsassociation.org.

78. Wespath Benefits and Investments, *2020 Annual Report*, 17.

79. Pension Fund of the Christian Church, "History."

80. Smietana, "More Than $90 Million" (*Washington Post*). In 2022, a class action lawsuit was filed against the AME Church alleging mismanagement of retirement funds. See L. Blair, "AME Church"; Poole, "AME Church Uncovers"; Smietana, "More Than $90 Million" (*Religion News Service*); Terrell, "AARP Foundation Aims"; Department of Retirement Services, "Important Update."

81. General Board of Pension and Health Benefits of the United Methodist Church, *Century of Caring*, 4.

82. Church Pension Fund, "Statement of the Board."

Mutual traces its history back to 1917 with the founding of the Brotherhood Aid Association, which "insured farms, homes, mercantile properties, and church buildings."[83] As they expanded, they incorporated, became autonomous from their denomination, and in 1972 made the decision to focus solely on providing insurance to church buildings and operations.[84] "Today, Brotherhood Mutual insures more than 65,000 churches and related ministries."[85] Church Mutual was founded even earlier in 1897 as Wisconsin Church Mutual Fire Insurance Association to provide insurance to churches, particularly in the event of fires.[86] As they expanded beyond the state of Wisconsin and provided more than just insurance for fires, they rebranded to Church Mutual Insurance Company. Now they operate in all fifty states, have about $2.2 billion in assets, and are "the leading insurer of religious organizations of all denominations."[87]

Insurance companies like these have an interest in clergy and church well-being. Brotherhood Mutual and Church Mutual each invest significantly into programs supporting clergy health in a number of areas. For example, Brotherhood Mutual donated to Full Strength Network, a ministry that connects clergy to the caregivers they need.[88] Church Mutual, as one example, hosted a series of webinars during the COVID-19 pandemic on various health topics for pastors.[89]

Denominationally-linked pension and benefits boards also support programs for clergy, such as in continuing education, retreats, and conferences. The Pension Fund launched their Excellence in Ministry program in 2015 in partnership with the Lilly Endowment to provide financial management training to new pastors and to instruct them on the theology of money and stewardship.[90] The Church Pension Group and the Board of Pensions of the PC(USA) sponsor wellness conferences for their clergy, called CREDO conferences, that have been held since the mid-1990s.[91]

83. Brotherhood Mutual, "Bearing One Another's Burdens."

84. Brotherhood Mutual, "Bearing One Another's Burdens."

85. Brotherhood Mutual, "Who We Are."

86. Church Mutual Insurance Company, "About Us."

87. Church Mutual Insurance Company, "About Us."

88. Brotherhood Mutual, "Brotherhood Mutual Donates $500,000."

89. Church Mutual Insurance Company, email to authors, September 22, 2021.

90. Pension Fund of the Christian Church, "Excellence in Ministry."

91. Church Pension Group, "About CREDO."

Wespath has historically hosted a Church Benefits Academy for clergy nearing retirement and "Revitup!" events for young clergy.[92]

Frontline Providers

The sector of "frontline providers" includes individuals and organizations dedicated to serving clergy who operate independently of denominations. This sector includes a variety of providers who often offer one-on-one care such as spiritual directors, counselors, coaches, therapists. Frontline providers also include those associated with resource centers and retreat centers.[93] Some are part of large organizations, while others operate with one or two persons on staff. We find that these types of providers have a similar orientation in the care they offer to clergy.

Spiritual Direction, Counseling, and Coaching

In the Christian tradition, much of the history of spiritual direction can be traced back to monastic formation, with novice monks working under the guidance of more experienced monks.[94] The Roman Catholic tradition has continuously held that those called to priesthood need a spiritual director due to the nature and demands of their career.[95] Protestant theologian Eugene Peterson agrees. As part of a larger movement to recover lost spiritual disciplines at the end of the twentieth century, Peterson writes, "It is not merely nice for pastors to have a spiritual director; it is indispensable."[96]

The growth of modern spiritual direction as a field is a small part of a larger movement that also includes coaching and counseling programs. The lines between spiritual direction, coaching, and counseling can be blurry, especially when the coaching and counseling is named as expressly Christian. A simplified way of distinguishing the fields is based on the particular

92. In response to COVID, the information and resources shared during these programs moved into an online format in the event "Delivered to You."

93. Resource centers refer to centers within universities or seminaries and to similar organizations that compile research, tools, programs, and services for pastors. They are twice as likely to experience resistance compared to other organizations that provide care for clergy.

94. Wall, "Direction, Spiritual."

95. Merton, "Spiritual Direction."

96. Peterson, *Working the Angles*, 167.

focus and purpose of the program. Counseling tends to deal with the past and present, working within the field of psychology. Spiritual direction is a spiritual practice of learning in the present. Coaching works on creating plans for the present and future and is often focused on professional success or a "fulfilled life."[97]

Christian counseling emerged as an integration of Christianity and psychology in the late 1960s and early 1970s, with Jay Adams and Gary Collins as the most prominent figures in the early part of this movement.[98] Adams wrote the foundational document *Competent to Counsel* in 1970, and by 1980 Collins wrote a number of works, including *Christian Counseling: A Comprehensive Guide*.[99] The American Association of Christian Counselors (AACC), currently the largest network of Christian counselors, was founded by Gary Collins in 1986, and he also served as its first president.

A number of other important figures in Christian counseling began their own practices or associations in the 1970s and 1980s, but most were independent and have since ceased operations or never grew to have the same impact as the AACC.[100] Currently, the AACC is comparable in size to many secular professional organizations in the field of psychology with more than 50,000 members in its network of counselors and coaches. Unlike AACC, most other Christian counseling networks, such as the American Association of Pastoral Counselors (AAPC), have dwindled in size and claim fewer than 2,000 members.[101] The AAPC enfolded into the Association for Clinical Pastoral Education in 2019 as part of their Psychotherapy Commission, which operates as a "multi-disciplinary, multi-faith" group.[102]

Christian coaching is an even more recent development that also stems from the work of Gary Collins. His book, *Christian Coaching: Helping Others Turn Potential into Reality*, was published in 2001. It pioneered the integration of the rapidly expanding field of "life coaching" that developed

---

97. Scalise, "What Is Christian Life Coaching?"

98. Marrs, "Christian Counseling," 31–32. While both Adams and Collins had critiques of Freudian psychoanalysis, Collins attempted to integrate the fields of Christianity and psychology while Adams primarily sought to use the Bible to counsel people. This distinction is sometimes noted as the distinction between "Christian counseling" and "biblical counseling."

99. Marrs, "Christian Counseling," 31–32.

100. Marrs, "Christian Counseling," 32–33.

101. Marrs, "Christian Counseling," 32.

102. Action Alliance, "Resource."

in the 1990s with Christian values and ethical principles.[103] Life coaching is the second fastest growing profession after information technologies and, according to a 2020 study by the International Coaching Federation (ICF), there are over 70,000 certified life coaches worldwide.[104]

Both Christian coaches and counselors can seek board certification from a number of professional boards, including the International Board of Christian Care (IBCC), to verify their level of training and experience in the field and to certify that they are receiving continuing education.[105] However, professional counselors, including Christian counselors, must be licensed by a state-run board to operate in an area and charge for their services, while coaches currently face very few restrictions or regulations and do not require state licensing or certification.[106] Many Christian coach training programs direct students to seek credentialing as a life coach from the ICF, while others look for certification specifically in Christian life coaching as provided by organizations like the International Christian Coaching Institute (ICCI).[107]

Providers who offer coaching often do so in conjunction with other services, such as spiritual direction or retreats. While pastors can seek help from any Christian counselors or coaches, or even non-Christian ones, a few organizations and associations offer specialized care for clergy that addresses the unique issues they might face in ministry. Examples of coaching programs specific to pastors include SOULeader and PastorServe.

SOULeader offers coaching to help pastors get through a number of difficulties in ministry, such as transition, visioning, new church planting, and leadership development.[108] It also has general life coaching, focused on personal growth and emotional and spiritual health. Planning for sabbaticals and retreats is also offered by their program along with peer and support groups of pastors.[109] PastorServe also has both personal and professional coaching for pastors. It offers specialized coaching to help ministry

---

103. Scalise, "What Is Christian Life Coaching?"

104. Scalise, "What Is Christian Life Coaching?"

105. International Board of Christian Care, "FAQ."

106. International Board of Christian Care, "FAQ"; Scalise, "What Is Christian Life Coaching?"

107. International Christian Coaching Institute, "Three Levels of Credentialing."

108. SOULeader Resources, "Personal, Group & Team Coaching."

109. SOULeader Resources, "Personal, Group & Team Coaching."

leaders and their churches overcome specific issues, and even performs church assessments to make recommendations for future planning.[110]

Counseling for pastors tends to be offered by small, independent practices specializing in just that area of care, although a few networks exist. Full Strength Network offers a membership plan for pastors and ministry leaders that gives them affordable access directly to counseling and coaching. These services would cost hundreds to thousands of dollars more outside of the program depending on frequency of use. After seeing the need, Brotherhood Mutual helped provide funding for the creation of this network in 2015.[111]

Retreat Centers

The biblical foundations for the principles of rest and retreat find their source in God's rest on the seventh day of creation. As early Christian communities formed, some looked for retreat in the solitude of deserts or monastic communities.[112] However, retreat became a prominent spiritual discipline and required rule of practice by St. Ignatius of Loyola.[113] In the Roman Catholic tradition, retreat as a spiritual discipline was originally reserved for clergy, although the practice has been expanded to include laity with time. In the Protestant tradition, retreat has always been practiced by both clergy and laity alike.

In North America, camp meetings and revivals, as popularized by Methodists and the Stone-Campbell movement, were some of the first organized places for retreat.[114] By the 1850s, interest in seeking solitude in nature became a cultural phenomenon, in particular because of the transcendentalist movement and Henry David Thoreau's *Walden*. Unlike the large crowds found at camp meetings and revivals, the concept of a solitary retreat into nature, in the example of Thoreau's own retreat, would provide a space for rest and an independent journey to discover God. This model of retreat, however, was not just about rest, but also included seeking an experience with God or nature in an environment away from an increasingly industrialized society.

110. PastorServe, "Pastor Focused Coaching."
111. See https://fullstrength.org/about/.
112. Debuchy, "Retreats."
113. Debuchy, "Retreats."
114. Brown, "Finding America's Oldest."

In the late nineteenth and early twentieth centuries, retreat centers began opening across the United States, especially by denominations. By the mid-twentieth century, a professional association, which eventually became known as the Christian Camp & Conference Association, emerged to help support and oversee retreat ministry.[115] As counseling and psychology developed as respected fields, they became useful for clergy care alongside mental health care for all people. Seeing it as a significant need, a number of retreat centers focused on counseling opened, such as Marble Retreat in 1974.[116]

In our analysis, we have identified relatively few camp or retreat centers owned or operated by persons of color. We believe that this disparity relates to historical issues of economic and social inequality that have directly impacted landholding, concepts of work, leisure, and rest, and lack of transportation to rural locations, which may—at times—be limiting to persons of color.

Besides retreat centers offering counseling, some retreats simply offer space for a sabbath. These include cabins, bed-and-breakfast style accommodations, or even guest rooms in personal homes. There are a range of types of retreat centers a pastor might find, from retreats without any form of direction or programming to retreats that offer significant programs and counseling services that the pastor is expected to attend.

Today, with declining denominational support, isolated centers struggle to make ends meet. In our research, we came across many retreat centers that no longer actively kept up their websites or who have closed permanently. Unsurprisingly, there have been a number of retreat centers that closed for the foreseeable future due to the impact of the COVID-19 pandemic.

Continuing Education

The "continuing education" sector provides ongoing education to clergy post-seminary. The education offered may result in a formal degree or certification or be offered informally as a one-off workshop or seminar. In some settings, this type of education is referred to as "lifelong learning." Within the North American context, the need to educate clergy served as the single most important reason for opening colleges in the colonial era.[117] In 1634, the residents of the Massachusetts Bay Colony feared that they might "leave

115. Christian Camp & Conference Association, "Vision-Mission-Values."
116. See https://marbleretreat.org.
117. Brubacher and Rudy, *Higher Education in Transition*.

an illiterate Ministry [sic] to the Churches" when their current ministers died.[118] Therefore, they resolved to establish Harvard College to train their clergy. Similarly in Connecticut, Yale College President Thomas Clap proclaimed: "Colleges are Societies of Ministers for training up persons for the work of the *Ministry*."[119] As America grew, its commitment to religious education did also. Settlers to the Midwest believed that religious education had the power to tame the wild American frontier by instilling morality and Christian character within the region's fast-growing populace.[120]

Unlike the colonial era focus on educating clergy, the mission of many historically Black colleges and universities (HBCUs) empowered and uplifted Blacks through training that would lead to economic and social empowerment.[121] The education of Black clergy was a significant, but not always primary, goal of HBCUs. As seminaries that later developed into larger universities, such as Howard University or Hood Theological Seminary, HBCUs spawned the creation of many organizations and conferences specifically for the advancement of Black clergy. One of the oldest and largest of these gatherings is the Hampton University Ministers' Conference, which began in 1914. This conference played a significant role in gathering Black clergy during the civil rights movement and continues to be an influential gathering today.[122]

Before 1750, half of America's college students were preparing for the ministry. With the exception of the great revivals, this figure dropped steadily over the next 150 years until, by 1900, only 6.5 percent of students were studying religion.[123] Prior to World War I, divinity schools were at least equal to, if not leading, other university professional schools in funding. For example, Harvard Divinity School had more endowment funds than any other professional school at Harvard, besides the medical school, which had comparable funding. However, after the world wars, these other professional school programs grew much faster than divinity schools and quickly overshadowed them in terms of both enrollment and funding.[124]

118. Eliot, *New Englands* [sic] *First Fruits*, 23.

119. Geiger, *History*, 36–37.

120. Watkins, *Christian Theological Seminary, Indianapolis*, 1.

121. Albritton, "Educating Our Own," 314–15.

122. Hafiz, "LOOK."

123. Brubacher and Rudy, *Higher Education in Transition*, 10.

124. Mullin, "Review of *Hurrying toward Zion*," 408.

In the mid-twentieth century, the Association of Theological Schools (ATS) and the National Council of Churches (NCC) commissioned the first survey of continuing education for clergy. In his 1960 report, Connolly C. Gamble Jr. wrote:

> Any realistic evaluation of the present situation must acknowledge readily that many programs are and have been for years serving effectively in the continuing education of ministers. Yet it seems clear that these programs . . . do not satisfy the educational needs. Too many programs are not correlated with the tasks of the ministry. Too few provide the means and stimulus for continuing scholarly engagement. The American parish minister needs a study program, not merely an occasional educational contact. He needs a study program in which he grapples with theological issues. He needs sustained systematic study, continued in the face of difficulties.[125]

In response to the difficulties and deficits presented in this report, the NCC Department of the Ministry created a Committee on Continuing Education, which then established the Society for the Advancement of Continuing Education for Ministry (SACEM) in 1967 with Connolly Gamble as its first president. SACEM was designed as a network for "theological educators, program directors, consultants, program designers and brokers, and advocates of continuing education for ministry."[126] It continues today under the name ALLLM, the Association of Leaders in Lifelong Learning in Ministry.

During the same time frame, divinity schools began to develop doctor of ministry (DMin) programs, which culminated in ATS accrediting its institutions to award the DMin degree in 1970.[127] Gamble's 1960 report catalyzed these efforts, providing vision for the development of continuing education programs in the following decades. Continuing education for clergy did exist prior to 1960. For instance, Gamble recognized the Chautauqua conferences, twentieth-century summer institutes for ministers held at both public universities and theological schools, the opening of the College of Preachers in 1929, and clinical pastoral education programs beginning in the 1930s as significant antecedents to his own work.[128]

125. Gamble, *Continuing Theological Education*, 67.
126. D. Roberts, "Society for the Advancement."
127. Association for Doctor of Ministry Education, "History."
128. Gamble, "Continuing Education for Ministry," 2–3.

In addition to the DMin, new study and experience-based programs developed in the wake of Gamble's report, such as field education for clergy. Yet, many historic continuing programs also fell away. Most notably, in the 1960 survey, twenty-three state-supported universities reported holding continuing education programs for ministers in various subjects as long as they did not address sectarian doctrines.[129]

Despite the advancement and growth of further educational opportunities for clergy, as exemplified by the doctor of ministry program and the Association for Doctor of Ministry Education (ADME) to support such programs in 1990,[130] continuing education networks peaked in membership in the 1970s and 1980s. Afterward, these associations experienced a rapid decline in interest and membership. This is the case with ALLLM. ALLLM began a "re-visioning" process in 2011 to address a lack of interest in continuing education for clergy due to a lack of time and resources.[131] Among ALLLM's suggestions for new approaches to continuing education is a "peer to peer learning" approach through the creation of small communities of pastor-peers. Besides seeking to learn from each other, these peer groups were designed to address major issues in pastor care, such as loneliness and isolation, at the same time.[132]

The old model that sustained many seminaries is now breaking down. The financial support from many Christian denominations has not changed in the past twenty years; however, the cost of running these institutions has increased dramatically while the number of prospective students has decreased. In 2015, Andover Newton Seminary, the oldest graduate theological institution in America, announced plans to close, merging with Yale Divinity School. Over the preceding ten years, the student body had dropped by 50 percent. Over that same time period, Andover Newton experienced a budget shortfall of $1 million or more each year.[133] In this case, the choice to affiliate with a larger university in exchange for much-needed resources is

---

129. Gamble, *Continuing Theological Education*, 44.

130. Association for Doctor of Ministry Education, "History."

131. Society for the Advancement of Continuing Education for Ministry, "SACEM—AGM 2015 Minutes."

132. Society for the Advancement of Continuing Education for Ministry, "SACEM—AGM 2015 Minutes."

133. MacDonald, "Oldest US Graduate Seminary."

seen as a better approach than closing altogether. Regretfully, other schools are facing similar challenges and may be forced to merge or close.[134]

Theological schools for clergy have been challenged and supported toward finding new and innovative approaches to clergy education through grant opportunities provided by foundations including the Lilly Endowment. As one example, the Lilly Endowment's Pathways for Tomorrow Initiative issued grants to strengthen existing theological schools' programs that support clergy. The initiative also offered further grants for development of new or existing models of education that can be sustainable for the future of clergy training.[135] New pathways are already emerging beyond just receiving an MDiv degree from a seminary. Continuing education programs now include online courses and conferences, certificates, and non-degree programs. There is also an increase in parachurch entities that provide training for clergy, such as the Lake Institute on Faith and Giving.

Conclusion

These five diverse sectors constitute the large-scale network that supports clergy in the United States and Canada. Each sector has its own history that has informed its present day interests, programs, and services. The organizations represented within each sector vary by location, size of staff and budget, and specific scope of work. Yet, collectively, these individuals and organizations form the support network upon which many clergy rely to meet their needs. Each invests time, money, and energy providing programs or services that influence or directly support clergy. Most importantly, every sector has a stake in the well-being of clergy and consequently the church.

In light of their common investments and shared ministry focus, these sectors do sometimes overlap. For instance, a pension/benefit organization may be denominationally affiliated and offer continuing education courses, or a retreat center may offer continuing education courses. Yet, more often, we find that these sectors are siloed within their own area of expertise, denominational or theological traditions, or among grantee networks. While professional associations exist in each of the sectors we have addressed, they too show relatively little engagement across sectors.

The example of the situation in Haiti following the 2010 earthquake offers a warning to the network of clergy care providers of what can happen

---

134. Silliman, "Facing Financial Challenges."

135. Lilly Endowment, "Pathways for Tomorrow Initiative."

when there is a lack of strategic coordination between individuals and organizations addressing the same crisis. Organizations formed by separate historical precedents, priorities, and areas of focus have different priorities and approaches to the task at hand. In Haiti, each NGO entered the country with its own understanding of the problems it was there to address. Each NGO had its own strengths, motivations, and prior journey informing its approach. They came in with blinders on, laser-focused on the immediate consequences of the earthquake, indifferent to the companions in the field on either side of them approaching the devastation differently but tasked with the same assignment.

Unfortunately, this siloed approach to fixing short-term problems had long-term consequences for the Haitian people. Similarly, if the sectors of clergy care providers continue to operate mostly without cross-sector collaboration, clergy and church will experience long-term consequences. Each sector plays an important role in the legacy of clergy care in the church and society—historically, as well as in the future. From the individual who invests money in the field to the continuing education provider, as well as the coach or licensed marriage and family therapist, collectively, this network of providers contains a wealth of history and expertise to care for clergy. They need to collaborate.

3

The Making of a Clergy Care Provider

RON SERVED AS A pastor for twenty-two years before he dealt with burnout. It started as a simple hand tremor. As his family worried about Parkinson's disease, Ron sought advice from neurologists and psychologists. After testing, Ron was diagnosed with continuous traumatic stress disorder (CTSD) resulting from his experience as a pastor. As part of recovery, Ron looked back over his years in ministry, cataloging every hurt and betrayal. Eventually, Ron and his wife left local church ministry so that he could fully heal. Now, Ron runs a retreat center providing evidence-based programs for clergy. These programs focus on the pressures, demands, and wounds of ministry.

Ron's story speaks to two key pieces in this chapter. First, like many clergy care providers, Ron is a former pastor. Second, the pastoral experience often involves similar patterns of hurt and betrayal. Unlike Ron, not all providers have the self-awareness, courage, wherewithal, or financial resources to go through months of recovery like Ron. Even if they do, not all choose to seek help. This chapter addresses the formational experiences shaping the network that cares for clergy, whom we have been calling "clergy care providers."

In the pages that follow, we examine the formational experiences, background, education, and credentials these providers rely upon to understand and make decisions about the clergy they serve. Proper formation and training are essential for any professional field. For those who care for clergy, training and formation build the toolbox for ministry, conceptually orient the provider, and potentially increase effectiveness.

Formation

Seventy percent of our participants have previous pastoral experience. Nearly all of the remaining 30 percent have family members or close friends who are clergy. Empirically, no characteristic has a more formative impact across the sectors than previous pastoral experience. Ministerial experience forms a communal bond among those who know the joys and sorrows of service to the local church. You might think of this phenomenon as analogous to the way that some of the most ardent supporters of veterans' causes are veterans, veteran families, and friends of veterans. When someone knows what it is like to serve in the trenches, the likelihood that they will become a supporter of those in a similar context increases dramatically.

Some participants shared that prior pastoral service helped them better meet the needs of clergy. Consider Ted, who served as a pastor of First Baptist Church for thirty-nine years and now supports his denomination by caring for pastors in his region. Reflecting upon his time in local church ministry, Ted said, "[My ministry] experience has allowed me to walk with pastors as well as serve them." Ted's previous pastoral experience provided him with a unique wisdom, insight, and understanding into the life and ministry of a pastor. For Ted, he sees his years serving as a local pastor as what qualifies him to now serve others in the same role.

A Black psychologist, Shirley, noted that pastoral experience can be instrumental in providing a language that can foster trust. Particularly among communities of color, Shirley shared that a lack of equitable access to professional help has resulted in distrust of professionals. Previous pastoral experience can foster confidence in the programs or services a clergy care provider offers. Consider Frank, who became a clergy care provider after serving as a pastor of a nondenominational church for thirty years. He said, "Many pastors in the community and the region sought me out for personal care, often because I was 'safe' by not being affiliated with any denomination." Frank believes his experience in pastoral ministry gives him the legitimacy to care for clergy, while his service in a nondenominational context made him a trusted voice.

Prior ministry experience can help clergy care providers empathize with the unique challenges of ministry. We find this theme to be especially pronounced within counseling practices. Counselors often draw on their previous pastoral experience to establish rapport with clergy. Ron, whom we met in the introduction of this chapter, felt frustrated with the first few counselors he saw. They did not understand his experience as a pastor, and he said this lack of understanding delayed his recovery. Seeing a counselor who had served as a pastor and could empathize with his experiences made a difference in Ron's healing.

Pastoral Experience by Sector

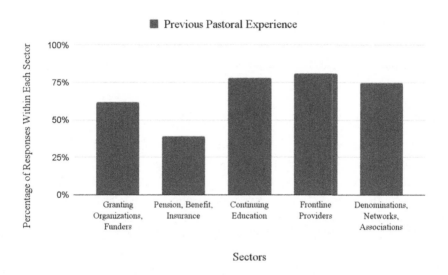

Figure 3–1: Pastoral Experience by Sector

Figure 3–1 shows the percentage of participants within each sector who have previous pastoral experience. Those in the pension, benefit, and insurance providers sector stand out as the least likely to have previous pastoral experience. With only 40 percent of pension, benefit, and insurance providers having served in a pastoral role, this sector is nearly a third less likely than the other sectors to have previous pastoral experience. Frontline providers, continuing educators, and those in denominational roles are much more likely to have served in pastoral ministry. Inside the frontline providers sector, counselors are the most likely to have previous pastoral experience. With more than 80 percent of counselors reporting previous pastoral experience, counselors are statistically three times more likely than those in other sectors to have previous pastoral experience.

For pension, benefit, and insurance providers, the relative lack of previous pastoral experience may represent a disadvantage. Providers in this sector may not fully understand the experiences or needs of clergy. On the other hand, pension, benefit, and insurance providers bring a variety of backgrounds and experiences to their work. From actuaries and lawyers to physicians and counselors, this diversity of expertise may contribute to the creation of more integrated and holistic programs. Stated differently, sectors with more previous pastors have less diversity in background and expertise. As one of our advisors questioned, "Could it be that the high degree of previous pastors is not a benefit but a liability?" In some cases, the best option for clergy support may be to have providers who have a passion for those in ministry but with professional training and experience from different backgrounds.

Shadow Side

In her book *Feed My Shepherds*, author and United Church of Christ pastor Flora Wuellner describes a time when she no longer felt joy in her ministry. More intentional prayer did not lead her to greater satisfaction. Although she continued to faithfully serve those around her, inwardly, her actions felt empty and disingenuous. With time, Flora discovered her problem resulted from wounds she received in her ministry. These wounds corroded the joy and satisfaction she found in ministry. She concludes, "I did not trust God with the 'shadow side' of much of my unfaced, unacknowledged inner self."[1]

At best, previous pastoral experience builds rapport, develops empathy, fosters trust, and equips clergy care providers with a deep understanding of the clergy they serve. At worst, trauma in pastoral ministry may lead to a "shadow side." When a provider has untreated wounds from their previous ministry, their care can become not only ineffective but also detrimental. Since more than two-thirds of clergy care providers have previous pastoral experience, it begs the question of what their pastoral experience was like.

Marie's husband Mike was a pastor in a reformed denomination. When Mike entered pastoral ministry as a second career, the entire family made

---

1. See Wuellner, *Feed My Shepherds*, 24–25. Also, traumatic experience prior to service in pastoral ministry may also lead to a shadow side.

sacrifices to accept the calling. After serving the local church (without a pay raise) for more than seven years, Marie's family went through a series of traumatic experiences as a powerful contingent of laity pushed their family out of the church. Each family member was hurt, but Mike was devastated. Mistreated by the church, he left the ministry to pursue a different career. Marie told herself that she would do something to ensure that other families would not have to experience what her family went through. Now, Marie oversees clergy care for the more than 2,500 ministers in her denomination.

A number of pastors experience burnout or trauma during their careers. Dr. Matt Bloom, the director of the University of Notre Dame's Wellbeing at Work project, which has studied clergy well-being, has found that more than one in three pastors across multiple denominations report experiencing significant burnout during their ministry.[2] While previous pastoral experience may help providers relate to and understand the experiences of clergy, their professional background may also be filled with trauma, burnout, and other negative experiences. If providers of clergy care have not done the work to find healing, these experiences can have a detrimental effect on their ability to provide care.

For more than two decades, Randy has worked at a resource center specializing in conflict mediation for clergy. In his experience working with denominational officials and alongside other providers, Randy has found that many of those who care for clergy have either been burned out or beaten up by the local church. The church, in general, does not have clear options for the many clergy who want to heal their wounds. With unresolved trauma, these providers minister not out of their healing but out of their woundedness.

Randy must discern whether the people he hires to care for clergy have an authentic calling because he has found that, for some, supporting clergy is a way of exerting control over those in ministry. When Randy gets a call from someone who wants to provide care for pastors, he asks himself, "Is this a call or an escape? Is this their way of getting out of ministry or is it a deeper call into ministry?" The same tendencies to abuse power that may have led some to leave local church ministry can be applied in the midst of clergy care, harming those who turn to them for help and guidance.

Our research confirms Randy's observation. In many of our interviews, we asked our participants to share their story of why and how they became clergy care providers. For most, it started with a story of: "I was

2. Bloom, "Burning Out in Ministry."

a pastor, and then, I went through a season of burnout." Sometimes our participants shared how members in their congregation betrayed them or hurt their family. They told us stories of facing surprising rejection and lies from cruel, vindictive people. In a few cases, our participants openly wept when describing the pain they experienced.

Trauma may also be present before an individual enters congregational ministry. Research from Duke University's Seminary to Early Ministry study reveals a concerning trend among master of divinity students who enter their program with previous traumatic experiences.[3] Consider these findings:

- One in ten incoming students lived with someone who was suicidal or abused drugs prior to the age of eighteen.
- One in five students had lived with someone who abused alcohol.
- Nearly one in three lived with someone who had been diagnosed with a form of mental illness.
- Half of the students had experienced an adult who insulted or swore at them.
- One in five had experienced unwanted sexual contact.

Not everyone has past trauma or a shadow side. However, we have found Randy's concern to be frequently confirmed not only in our interviews but also in outside research. Our participants express concern about those who have exited local church ministry with significant wounds. Given the lack of formal training to provide care for clergy and the concerns many of our participants noted, we believe it important to pay attention to the potential harmful implications in the field of clergy care.

It is not necessarily problematic that clergy have traumatic experiences.[4] So long as clergy have access to safe individuals *qualified* to offer care, they can take steps towards becoming healthier leaders. However, hidden, unexplored, or unaddressed trauma can be concerning. One of our participants described this process like receiving divorce counseling from someone who has unresolved issues from their own divorce. We find that pastors may cover up previous trauma, trying to maintain the image that they "have it all together" or thinking that others deserve more help than they do. One participant, a licensed psychologist and professor of pastoral

3. Eagle et al., "Seminary to Early Ministry."
4. See Nouwen, *Wounded Healer*.

counseling, shared a story of a pastor who had fallen into this trap, which led to unhealthy dynamics with the staff and the congregation. People left the church feeling used because the pastor was controlling others rather than working through their own trauma.

Providers with a shadow side can cause more harm than good. We interviewed Kirk, a professor of psychology on the West Coast of the United States. Kirk shared a story of a kind, well-meaning individual named Thomas who had been through a period of ministry burnout. Now, Thomas provides support to pastors through a nondenominational organization. Kirk said:

> I did not get the sense that [Thomas] had sought professional help or really processed his burnout. He also implied that his burnout experience was the thing that qualified him to help other clergy. He did not have any theological higher education degrees, counseling credentials/licenses, or coaching certification.... One of the pastoral couples he was helping had been through multiple episodes of infidelity on the part of the husband. The couple had not been referred to marital therapist, sexual addiction treatment for clergy, etc. I was concerned that given the severity and complexity of something like this in a marriage, he may unintentionally be doing harm rather than helping.

Kirk's story illustrates the concern of the cyclical nature of the shadow side. When wounded providers "care" for hurting clergy, they may improperly treat, provide for, refer, or counsel ministers in need. They are like a surgeon with a broken arm trying to set the broken bone of another. Their actions may exacerbate injuries and lead to lasting consequences. To make matters worse, clergy who are treated by those with unresolved issues may care for others in the same way they have experienced care. The cycle continues until disrupted by better care, healing, or accountability.

Calling

Calling also plays a significant role in shaping the formative experience of providers. More than 90 percent of our participants agree that God has called them to care for clergy as part of their ministry. Those with previous pastoral experience are more than twice as likely to agree that God has called them to care for pastors when compared to those without pastoral experience. Calling can be a valuable resource for those in ministry. As one interviewee, Peter, who led a retreat center stated: "My wife and I would never have become involved in this work unless there was a clear-cut call from God. . . . In tough times, it comes back to calling." For Peter, calling provides assurance. At the same time, he was also aware that calling does not necessarily mean that caring for clergy is what anyone with a ministerial calling should do.

How does calling impact the shadow side? It may be one reason that some feel unable to leave "the ministry" after a traumatic experience. Samantha is a young professional who has worked on a number of statewide clergy care projects. She said:

> The word calling has been one of the main reasons I've stayed in situations that . . . made me uncomfortable, situations that harmed me, didn't align with my beliefs, [and] made me feel exasperated anxiety or depression.

Samantha went on to explain that she stayed in these situations because she felt that she was supposed to suffer for Christ.

Sue, who works in theological education, discussed the tension between calling and caring. She has experienced students whose psychological profiles and field education experiences indicated that they were not in a healthy place to move forward in ministry. Nevertheless, the students have insisted that they were "called," and on a number of occasions, field education sites have provided these students with positive assessments in order to protect the "calling" of these students. Calling was problematic in these situations because it overrode conversations about how to better care for these students or how to protect those served by these students. Calling can be a source of comfort and motivation to care for clergy. It can provide encouragement when ministry is challenging, resources are few, or resistance is high. However, calling can also be problematic when it falsely draws people who are more likely to do harm than good.

Training

Beyond formation, training is also essential for clergy care providers. They possess a diverse set of training and credentials. These experiences range from those without formal training to academics with PhDs. They include licensed marriage and family therapists, certified coaches, and lawyers, just to name a few.[5] Some of our participants shared that they tried to stay "up to date on the latest research" related to clergy or sought additional certification in coaching or facilitation.

To investigate the training of the network, we asked our participants whether they had any formal or informal training to care for clergy. After these initial questions, we provided additional space for our participants to define for themselves what type of training they counted as formal or informal.[6] According to our participants, training can be "formally" understood as education, certification, and ministry experiences. "Informally," training relates to relationships with mentors, workshops, or on the job training. While many have advanced degrees, our data indicates a general lack of standardized training within the field.

The following table displays the percentages of our participants indicating they have (a) both formal and informal training, (b) only formal training, (c) only informal training, or (d) neither formal nor informal training. The good news is that more than half (51 percent) of our participants have both formal and informal training to provide care for clergy. However, just over one fourth (27 percent) do not have formal training. More concerning, one in ten (10 percent) have neither formal nor informal training.

Participant's Formal vs. Informal Training

		Do you have **informal** training?	
		Yes	No
Do you have **formal** training?	Yes	51%	12%
	No	27%	10%

Overall, 78 percent of providers rely on informal training to care for pastors. In fact, more of our participants indicate that they have informal

5. Many of our participants wear multiple hats. For example, one of our participants is a psychologist who both teaches seminary students and supports Black bivocational clergy.

6. In the network of providers, there is not a singular definition of how to distinguish between informal and formal training for clergypersons. We find that each sector has different understandings in whether it includes pastoral experience as formal or informal training or whether workshops are formal or informal training, for example.

training than formal training.[7] We celebrate these informal connections that ground the care provided to clergy. However, we are concerned about those without any formal training to care for clergy. In our sample, nearly one in three providers of clergy care rely on informal training alone. Figure 3–2 displays formal and informal training by sector.

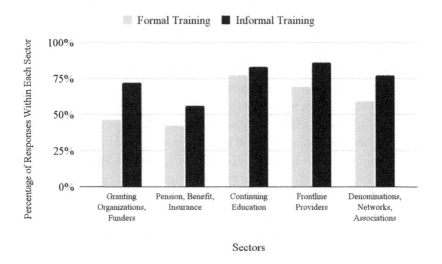

Figure 3–2: Formal and Informal Training by Sector

Our participants have various understandings of what counts as formal or informal training due to the specific expectations of their sector, previous experiences, and culture. For example, some of our Latinx participants did not include some of their expertise in our formal survey. However, we learned about their training through interviews. Some participants include advanced degrees they obtained in "other" fields, while others dismiss those degrees as irrelevant to their current work. Although one of our participants holds a terminal law degree, he does not see this degree as part of the formal training that equips him to care for clergy. Additionally, what one provider might consider informal training, another provider might consider formal training. Therefore, some overlapping categories between formal and informal training appear in the analysis that follows.

7. Some of the categories our participants used for informal training overlap with categories used for formal training indicating that the field may not have a clear sense of what constitutes formal vs. informal activity or the various ways that the same type of activity could take place in formal or informal contexts.

Formal Training

Figure 3–3 shows each category of formal training and the percentage of participants across sectors who listed it. Approximately two-thirds of our participants counted degrees or certificates as formal training. The sectors vary in the ways they count certain experiences as formal training to care for clergy. Each sector has a number of providers with advanced degrees as well as undergraduate degrees from Bible colleges. By a slight margin,[8] continuing education providers count more degrees as their formal training than other sectors. This is not surprising since many continuing education providers operate out of an academic setting where a degree may be required for employment. Many of the degrees they cite are DMins or PhDs.

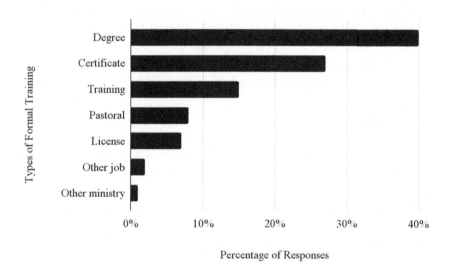

Figure 3–3: Types of Formal Training

The certificate category includes a variety of certifications, ranging from formal certificates offered in an academic institution to certificates for coaching.[9] Examples of organizations providing certification for our partici-

---

8. Twenty-eight percent of responses from the continuing education providers compared to 27 percent from the denomination, association, and network sector and 26 percent from the frontline providers' sector. However, considering that the continuing education providers are a smaller proportion of the field, the 28 percent of responses represents a disproportionate share of the responses.

9. The categories of training and certificate often overlapped in our participants'

pants include the John Maxwell Team, Coach U, and RightPath Leadership. Many of our participants hold certification by the ICF. As the coaching profession is relatively new and often lacks broad based standards and training requirements, we have found many providers who refer to themselves as "coaches" without completing any training or certification process. The ICF provides ethical guidelines for coaching along with certifications based on education and experience. However, some of our participants noted that, despite the guidelines offered by ICF and similar entities, there are still only a few mechanisms of accountability in the coaching subsector.

The granting organizations and funders sector and the pension, benefit, and insurance providers sector are less likely to rely on certificates as part of their formal training for clergy care than other sectors. A disproportionately smaller number of responses came from these sectors. Frontline providers and those who work in denominations, networks, and associations are more likely to rely on certificates than other sectors. One person we interviewed shared how he wanted a certificate in coaching because it provided a model for connecting with clergy and leading them through steps of recovery.

Fifteen percent of the responses to formal training included various forms of "training" such as conflict management, small group facilitation, or financial planning, to name a few. Continuing education providers stand out the most in their overrepresentation of the participants counting training as formal preparation to care for clergy. Distinct from those with certification, many included training to become a coach. Whether or not they earned a certification, they still considered the training a valuable experience that shapes the programs and services they provide.[10]

Across the network of providers, our participants consider pastoral experience an important part of their formal education.[11] A Lutheran care

---

answers. Here, training is an umbrella term that refers to various experiences our participants call "training." When our participants used "training" they referred to general experiences that shape who they are as clergy care providers.

10. The continuing education sector is more likely to point to a wide range of experiences as influential in how they care for clergy. In addition to previous pastoral experience, they also see a number of other experiences as providing important insights into how to care for clergy.

11. Our participants included pastoral experience as both formal and informal training. For some, pastoral experience was significant enough to be formal training and for others, they saw it only as the informal experiences that prepared them to care for clergy. Some included pastoral experience as part of both their informal and formal training to care for pastors. Since there is some variation in how each sector regards the "formality"

provider with whom we spoke agreed. He said, "We consider previous pastoral ministry experience to be the best training." More participants listed pastoral experience as part of their formal training than those who listed a license as part of their training to provide care.

Our results show that frontline providers and continuing education providers, in particular, believe that previous pastoral experience qualifies them to care for clergy. Frontline providers are especially more likely to have previous pastoral experience. They are people in their second (or third) career and caring for clergy is a natural extension of their previous ministry. Most of the people we spoke with who led retreats had previous pastoral ministry experiences. They had been through burnout and trauma and wanted to provide other pastors a place to escape and rejuvenate.

This is not to say that other sectors—particularly denominations, networks, and associations—do not also rely on their previous pastoral experience as formal training. Many of them do have previous pastoral experience. However, frontline providers and continuing education providers stand out as those who draw heavily upon their previous pastoral experience in their support of clergy.

One of the most dramatic differences among the sectors is illustrated in those who include a license as part of their formal training. Half of those who have a license are frontline providers; one in four are from the denominations, networks, and associations sector. Many frontline providers serve as counselors, licensed marriage and family therapists, or other similar professions. About 15 percent are licensed in their state to provide therapy and counseling. Unlike frontline providers, those in the denominations, networks, and associations sector often do not have the additional qualifications and accountability structures that come with licensure. Slightly fewer than 12 percent of continuing educators cite a license as part of their formal training. Many of those continuing educators with a license have their own counseling practice or the license is from a previous career.

The last category of formal training includes those who cited "other ministry" as part of their formal training. Distinct from "pastoral" ministry, other ministry includes non-pastoral experiences such as work within local congregations, denominational bodies, mission organizations, or other nonprofits. For example, these experiences consisted of work as Sunday School teacher, deacon, personal assistant, secretary, campus ministry, or

---

of previous pastoral experience, we maintained the distinction between formal and informal training.

missions work. While many of these individuals provide valuable care for people, we would like to know more about how and in what way these experiences qualify someone to care for clergy and if there may be better experiences available.

Not only do frontline providers disproportionately rely on previous pastoral experience but also on other ministry experiences. Although frontline providers constitute 34 percent of the network of providers we identified, they represented nearly 50 percent of the responses citing "other ministry" as informal training. Other ministry experiences can provide frontline providers with knowledge and understanding of the role and responsibilities of a clergyperson even though they themselves may not have personal pastoral experience. Particularly for women in denominations that do not ordain women, other ministry experiences can provide insight into the experiences of the clergy they care for and foster trust between the clergyperson and provider.

Informal Training

Our participants also consider a wide variety of experiences as informal training to care for clergy. Figure 3–4 illustrates the types of informal training our participants specified. Nearly 50 percent of our participants referred to previous (or sometimes current) pastoral experience as part of their informal training. The granting organizations and funders sector and the pension, benefit, and insurance providers sector are more likely than the other sectors to categorize previous pastoral experience as informal training. These sectors see pastoral experience as informative for their work, but not the formal training they need to support clergy.

After pastoral experience, workshops were the most frequently mentioned type of informal training. More than two-thirds of the responses in this category came from the denominations, networks, and associations sector and the continuing education provider sector.[12] Workshops can encompass several types of experiences. Some of our participants attend workshops for congregational leaders. Others attend workshops specifically

12. Given their access to training within the academy, we expected the continuing education sector as the most likely to cite workshops. Somewhat surprisingly, the denominations, networks, and associations sector overwhelms this form of informal training. Instead, more than 50 percent of the responses come from the denominations, networks, and associations sector and 20 percent comes from the continuing education sector.

related to clergy care or similar topics such as marriage, church planting, or leadership. Some of these workshops include professional development seminars hosted by faculty within their academic institutions or workshops hosted by organizations such as the American Association of Biblical Counselors.

Hardly any pension, benefit, or insurance providers specify workshops as part of their informal training.[13] When pension, benefit, or insurance providers refer to workshops as part of their informal training they point to conferences and seminars on church stewardship, planned gift administration, and related topics. While other sectors attend general workshops on clergy care or leadership, pension, benefit, and insurance providers are more likely to focus on the topics that are relevant to their own sector.

Participants also noted "other" ministry experiences. For instance, one individual mentioned serving as "an armor bearer," a position in some congregational settings that functions as an assistant to the pastor and sometimes is stationed as a bodyguard for the pastor. Curiously, some of our participants consider their degree or certificate as an experience of informal training. Many of these degrees included Bible college degrees or various professional degrees that were not directly related to their specific sector.

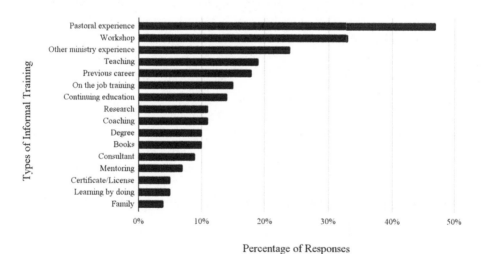

Figure 3–4: Types of Informal Training

13. Only 2 percent of responses.

Some providers have previous research and teaching experience. About 15 percent of our participants rely on research (either research that they personally conducted or others' research), continuing education courses, and teaching (often their own teaching) as informal experiences that shape how they care for clergy.[14] They also attend a number of gatherings that present the latest research on clergy trends such as ones hosted by their denomination, Caregivers Forum, and the Common Table Collaborative.

The denominations, networks, and associations sector depends more on informal training to care for clergy than other sectors. Nearly 40 percent of those relying on informal training work with denominations, networks, or associations, even though they comprise slightly fewer than 30 percent of the overall field. Given their relative proportion of the field, we would expect a greater percentage of frontline providers, continuing educators, and pension, benefit, and insurance providers to rely on informal training. However, we find that those sectors are less likely to consider informal training experiences as significant in their preparation to care for clergy.

Neither Formal nor Informal Training

Ten percent of our participants have neither formal nor informal training. Figure 3–5 compares those who have neither formal nor informal training to those with both formal and informal training by sector.

The most surprising contrast is in the percentage of pension, benefit, and insurance providers who have neither formal nor informal training. Although they are fewer than 10 percent of the field, they are disproportionately more than 20 percent of those with neither formal nor informal training.[15] And, while other sectors have more members with both formal and informal training, the pension, benefit, and insurance providers sector splits evenly between those with neither and those with both formal and informal training. To a lesser extent, granting organizations and funders also stand out in their proportion that have neither formal nor informal training.

14. Because only a small number of participants selected either research, continuing education, or teaching, we combined each category into one since they represent the academic sources of informal training.

15. More participants from the denomination, association, and network sector and the frontline providers sector have neither formal nor informal training, but that result is relatively comparable to their proportion within the field.

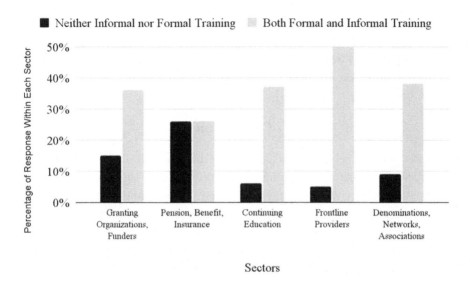

Figure 3–5: Comparison of No Training with Both Types of Training

We find that representatives from denominational foundations are less likely to believe that they care for clergy even though their responsibilities have an impact on the overall well-being of clergy. For instance, in multiple conversations with officials from denominational foundations, we heard the refrain, "It is not my job to care for clergy." The leaders in this sector are more likely to see their role as providing financial services for congregations and not support for clergy. Representatives from this sector often conclude that those in other sectors play a more important role supporting clergy. Yet, as they describe their ministry, we find they commonly discuss programs and services that help clergy to make wise personal and professional financial decisions, conduct capital campaigns, and manage their congregation's property, gifts, and other assets.

This dynamic affects how they think of their own education and training and whether those experiences matter in the ways they care for clergy. The pension, benefit, and insurance providers, and the granting organizations and funders in our sample are highly educated with a wealth of experience to perform their respective functions. They differ from other sectors in that they do not see those experiences as important in caring for clergy.

More than 50 percent of our overall sample have both formal and informal training. A disproportionate number of frontline providers and continuing educators cite both formal and informal training. Overall, continuing educators and frontline providers are more likely to connect their training and formation to the care they provide for clergy. They draw on a wider variety of experiences to inform their work which could affect the types of programs and services they provide.

Conclusion

Pastoral ministry serves not only as the background of most providers but also as their formative orientation to clergy care. This is a network of clergy, for clergy, and by clergy. From their pastoral experience, providers learn what ministry is like, how to relate to others in ministry, and gain knowledge that cannot be found in a textbook. Indeed, previous pastoral experience is the single most defining feature of the clergy care provider network. And, tragically, many have the scars to prove it. The number of untreated traumatic experiences associated with pastoral ministry among clergy care providers raises alarms. The combination of untreated ministry wounds and a lack of standardized training or certification for providers may be substantial factors contributing to burnout and unhealthy clergy, both of which impact the culture and effectiveness of congregations.

In chapter 2, we highlighted the silos that exist among the network of clergy care providers, often by sector. Here again, we see a consequence of the disconnect. The formative experiences and training that shape clergy care are not equally distributed among the sectors. Some sectors have an abundance of degrees and continuing education opportunities to inform their understanding of the needs of clergy. Other sectors lack measures of accountability and credentialing. To some extent these differences are natural given the different professions and professional bodies of knowledge. Yet, we hope that the sectors can reach beyond their silos and share their expertise, experiences, and accountability measures with each other. Some sectors need to develop informal mechanisms for training and formation such as mentor relationships. Other sectors need to call for greater credentialing and oversight.

There are key strengths and significant pockets of expertise in this network. For example, 50 percent of clergy care providers rely on both formal and informal training. In addition to benefits of pastoral experience, a number of our participants draw on research, certification, licenses, continuing education, and additional readings. Standardizing the necessary requirements to care for clergy and establishing mechanisms of accountability will ensure the network progresses in the quality of care provided. While formalization of these experiences may be beneficial, we also acknowledge that formalization can exclude marginalized communities.[16] For instance, creating standards could emphasize the possession of certain skills or levels of education of which marginalized communities have historically been denied access.

Training and formational experiences provide the theoretical frameworks and practical tools that providers use in their ministry to clergy. They help to provide perspective to understand and overcome challenges, and they can—if properly stewarded—increase effectiveness of the programs and services provided. Exploring the training and experiences that form clergy care providers in each sector gives us a better sense of the strengths within the network, as well as opportunities for growth and collaboration. The following table details each sector's key strengths and opportunities from this chapter:

Formation and Training—Strengths and Opportunities

Sectors	Strengths	Opportunities
Frontline Providers	A number have previous pastoral experience. As counselors, therapists, and similar professionals, previous pastoral experience gives them legitimacy and builds trust with the clergy they care for. In addition to their previous pastoral experience, a number of frontline providers maintain and seek out formal credentials (such as counseling licenses) to care for clergy. These credentials establish mechanisms of accountability and trust with other professionals.	Despite these credentials, this sector also has a number who rely on certifications with few mechanisms of accountability. An opportunity for the establishment of a system of accountability and standardization of qualifications to care for clergy exists. Interdenominational accepted minimum standards for clergy care providers would protect clergypersons seeking help and minimize unhelpful care.

16. For an example, see Baines, "Race, Resistance, and Restructuring."

Formation and Training—Strengths and Opportunities

Sectors	Strengths	Opportunities
Denominations, Networks, and Associations	Similar to frontline providers, this sector's strength is in the value of previous pastoral experience and the trust and legitimacy such experiences lend to the relationships with the clergy for whom they care.	Denominations, networks, and associations are even less likely than frontline providers to rely on standardized qualifications such as licensing, suggesting ample opportunities for these organizations to establish clear expectations for the necessary qualifications to care for clergy.
Continuing Education Providers	We examined how this sector draws on a diversity of experiences, including advanced degrees. They combine both a number of informal experiences and formal degrees, which can be a valuable asset to the field of clergy care.	Since a number of continuing education providers have advanced degrees and additional formative experience, we see opportunities for them to share their expertise with other sectors. In particular, as we will detail in the next chapter, there is very little dialogue occurring between the academic community and other providers. Continuing education providers can spearhead conversations with other sectors through workshops, conferences, and other opportunities.
Pension, Benefit, Insurance Providers	This sector draws less on previous pastoral ministry and more on formal training for their careers in the profession. The greater diversity outside of pastoral ministry may lend itself to greater stability in the field (more rich perspectives and less susceptibility to the shadow side).	The pension, benefit, and insurance providers sector's uniqueness may make it more difficult for them to collaborate with others in the field. They are also less likely to have the pastoral experience that can provide them with credibility and trust from the clergy they serve.

Formation and Training—Strengths and Opportunities

Sectors	Strengths	Opportunities
Funders and Granting Organizations	In many ways, granting organizations and funders have similar formative experiences and outcomes as those in the pension, benefit, and insurance sector.	We see an opportunity for funders and granting organizations to examine how their core competencies, especially in the financial services, might support clergy in their ministries and the benefit that this could provide to their organizations.

4

_____

We Aren't Reading the Same Things

WE ARE A PRODUCT of our environment. What we consume shapes how we understand the world and respond to it. Everything from our preferred news outlets, family and friends, and the books we choose to read impacts us and, ultimately, the decisions we make. In the same way, clergy care providers are influenced by the information and sources they consult. The literature these providers consume shapes their understanding of clergy well-being. When one provider's literature differs from the literature another relies on, a sharp divergence of ideas, language, and practices develops.

We took an unconventional approach to reviewing the literature on clergy care. Instead of drawing on only a formal academic review of the literature concerning clergy care and clergy well-being, we also asked our participants about the sources that inform and inspire them in their work as providers. We did this because the academic literature alone is not the only information influencing clergy care. Other sources of literature influence how providers practically provide support to clergy. In this chapter, we compare these two sources impacting the field of clergy care today—the scholarly literature and the literature we learned our participants rely on in their work. Our comparison reveals major topics, contributions, and gaps found in each set of sources.

Comparison of Literatures

We discovered that the literature our participants consume varies significantly from the available scholarly literature and academic research. Our participants provided us with the titles of books, articles, and other materials that inspire and inform their work caring for clergy. We then searched for scholarly literature associated with clergy care. Our scholarly literature search produced 236 unique titles, while our participants listed a total of 289 unique titles.[1]

Despite the combined literatures totaling 525 sources, only three titles overlap. These titles are: *Flourishing in Ministry: How to Cultivate Clergy Well-Being; A Lifelong Call to Learn: Continuing Education for Religious Leaders*; and *The COACH Model for Christian Leaders*.[2] The first title, *Flourishing in Ministry*, discusses practical recommendations to improve clergy well-being and inspires a number of our participants in their goals for clergy. The second is an edited volume of essays written by continuing education providers and similar practitioners. The third is a practical guide that uses coaching insights to teach Christian leaders how to minister more effectively to their target audiences.

The other 522 titles are all unique. Half of the scholarly literature we reviewed addresses mental and emotional health issues, with the majority focusing on burnout. By contrast, 25 percent of the literature cited by our participants specifically addresses mental and emotional health and not burnout. This comparison highlights the significant progress made by academics in understanding risk factors that affect a clergyperson's mental and emotional well-being.[3] By far the most prolific academic author is Rae Jean Proeschold-Bell. Her work generally takes a holistic approach to clergy health, meaning that it encompasses the mental, physical, and spiritual needs of clergy. This approach is specifically true of an article that she co-authored, "A 2-Year Holistic Health and Stress Intervention: Results of an RCT in Clergy." Her other work primarily focuses on mental and emotional health topics that seek to understand burnout, occupational distress, and depression among clergy.[4]

1. We excluded the Bible from our analysis.

2. Bloom, *Flourishing in Ministry*; Reber and Roberts, *Lifelong Call to Learn*; Webb, *COACH Model*.

3. For example, see Milstein et al., "Prospective Study"; Edwards et al., "Relationship between Social Support."

4. Consider the following as examples: Proeschold-Bell et al., "Using Effort-Reward

Next in the academic realm, Leslie J. Francis has written a number of articles on clergy burnout in various denominations, including the PC(USA), Anglican, and Roman Catholic traditions. He is the eponymous author of the Francis Burnout Inventory used to measure clergy burnout as outlined in "Assessing Clergy Work-Related Psychological Health: Reliability and Validity of the Francis Burnout Inventory."[5] Authors Maureen Miner Bridges and Mark McMinn have also made significant contributions to the field of clergy care. Maureen Miner focuses on burnout and mental health, especially as a result of the occupational demands and stress of ministry. Mark McMinn primarily focuses on the relationship between psychologists and clergy, as well as the resources provided for clergy mental health by various Protestant denominations.

In comparison to the scholarly literature on clergy care, our participants cited different authors. After the Bible, they mentioned works by Matt Bloom and Peter Scazzero most frequently. Matt Bloom wrote *Flourishing in Ministry: How to Cultivate Clergy Well-Being,* which drew on research with clergy from several denominations.[6] Peter Scazzero wrote *Emotionally Healthy Spirituality: Unleash a Revolution in Your Life in Christ,* which addresses the importance of growing in emotional maturity as part of one's spiritual growth. Other frequently cited authors include Brené Brown's work on vulnerability, Rob Reimer's work on spiritual renewal, and David Benner's insights as a psychologist on spirituality.

After considering the initial contrast in the scholarly literature available versus the sources informing our participants' understanding of clergy care, we compiled the summaries of each book and article in order to better understand the major topics most likely to be covered. The following figures (4–1 and 4–2) display word clouds of these summaries.[7] Both sets of literature contain a number of references to the "church" and to "ministry," suggesting that both the scholarly and participants' literatures address the impact of healthy clergy on local congregations and the church more broadly. However, the word clouds show a significant contrast between the two sources.

Imbalance Theory"; Miles and Proeschold-Bell, "Overcoming the Challenges."

5. Francis et al., "Assessing Clergy."

6. This resource has informed studies of clergy well-being since its publication. For example, Jankowski et al., "Religious Leaders' Well-Being"; Kreis and Diaz, "Factors Cultivating Well-Being"; Sielaff et al., "Literature Review"; Andrews, "Designing a Program."

7. We excluded common words and limited the word clouds to only the words that appear fifty times or more across all sources.

Figure 4–1: Academic Word Cloud | Figure 4–2: Participants' Word Cloud

For instance, "health" and "burnout" feature prominently in the academic word cloud. However, "health" and "burnout" do not appear in the participants' word cloud. The scholarly literature focuses on clergy well-being while our participants' focuses on the leadership skills clergy need to do well in ministry. Our participants' sources contribute a wealth of information on "church" and "leadership" but less about what clergy need as individuals in order to thrive in a professional ministry context.

These substantive differences result in scholarly literature that can answer plenty of questions about burnout but have much less to say about other aspects of clergy well-being and church leadership. In fact, almost one in three of our participants' sources were not explicitly Christian texts. Instead, 21 percent of the sources our participants provided address the general topic of "leadership," while only 5 percent of the scholarly literature focuses there. This comparison underscores what many of our participants told us. They turn to resources outside of the church to inform how they provide clergy care, either because of the shortage of literature available to them that is distinctly Christian or because they find general or practical resources on leadership, spiritual health, or other topics more helpful.[8]

---

8. Some examples include O. Brown, *New Kind of Venture Leader*; Lewis et al., *Another Way*; Nouwen, *In Name of Jesus*; and Bevins and Dunwoody, *Healthy Rhythms for Leaders*.

Indeed, 34 percent of our participants referenced practical ("how-to") literature, while only 1 percent of the scholarly literature we examined could be considered practical. For example, some how-to books our participants mentioned offered steps to helping someone overcome anxiety or find peace. Another practical guide mentioned was *The Four Levels of Healing* by Shakti Gawain. This disparity in percentages of how-to books signals that clergy care providers are much more interested than academics in learning how to address ministry challenges with practical tools.

Literature Topics[9]

While the titles and summaries from our two sets of sources helped us to compare contributions and gaps around key topics like mental and emotional health and leadership, our surveys and interviews also highlighted topics that we used as guides to further examine both literatures. These additional topics include socio-cultural context, relationships, ministry challenges, financial challenges, conflict and polarization, trauma, spirituality, and coaching.

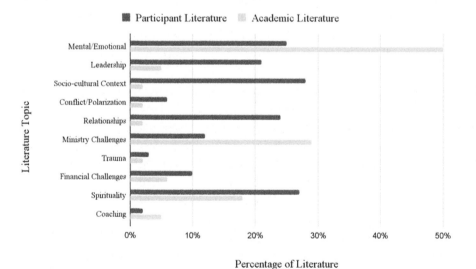

Figure 4–3: Topics Covered

9. We coded both literatures for common themes and compared the result to identify gaps in knowledge and practice. These themes were based on our participants' conceptualization of well-being (see ch. 4) and on other themes identified in our interviews.

For our participants, 28 percent of the literature they rely on addresses the socio-cultural context (e.g., issues such as racism and poverty). Books addressing the socio-cultural context range from neutral topics such as how to slow down and find Sabbath rest to more politically charged topics. The more politically engaged literature spans a spectrum of topics such as social justice or concerns about an increasingly pluralistic society. Examples of this type of literature include *The Politics of Ministry*; *A Secular Age*; and *After Whiteness: An Education in Belonging*.[10] Only 2 percent of the scholarly literature addresses the socio-cultural context. The articles in the scholarly literature examine clergy and their issues of mental health as a result of personality traits or job stressors, not about how societal factors shape their experiences in ministry.

Related, we coded the literature for resources addressing conflict and polarization to understand the theories and ideas that shape how our participants help clergy with handling conflict and polarization. Participants cited conflict and polarization as major stressors for pastors. Despite their concern, only 6 percent of our participants' literature specifically addresses conflict or polarization. The numbers are even lower for academic literature. Only 2 percent of the scholarly literature addresses conflict and polarization.

In our interviews, we found that many providers advocate for clergy developing trusting friendships outside of their congregations or denominational networks. In fact, some providers sponsor cohorts or peer support groups for clergy so that they have opportunities where these types of relationships can form. However, only 24 percent of the participants' literature directly addresses relationships—either as a general discussion of healthy relationships or, more specifically, relationships for pastors. For academics, only 2 percent of the literature addresses relationships. Our participants say that relationships matter for overall clergy well-being, but the scholarly literature often focuses on understanding the clergyperson in isolation.

Surprisingly, only 12 percent of the participants' literature specifically addresses the difficulties and challenges of ministry. We anticipated that this topic would be more concentrated in the participants' literature. However, the emphasis on ministry challenges is greater in the scholarly literature. There, the percentage jumps to nearly 33 percent. The scholarly community has provided increased attention to the difficulties and challenges of ministry.

10. Burns et al., *Politics of Ministry*; Jennings, *After Whiteness*; Taylor, *Secular Age*.

One such challenge is trauma. In our interviews with providers who previously served as pastors, our participants repeatedly mentioned either their own personal trauma from ministry or the trauma they see in the clergy they support. They emphasized that trauma and resilience were important concepts for the field in addressing clergy well-being. Despite this challenge rising to the surface in both our survey results and interviews, only 3 percent of the participants' literature and only 2 percent of the scholarly literature addresses trauma. David Wang, a professor of psychology and pastoral counseling and an expert on the topic of trauma informed care, confirmed that few resources on trauma specifically address clergy. This finding is especially interesting in light of the reality we noted earlier in the chapter that both sets of literature pay great attention to the mental and emotional health of clergy.

Many providers believe in the importance of financial management and financial well-being for clergy, and many offer services on these topics. However, only 10 percent of the participants' literature and only 6 percent of the scholarly literature specifically addresses financial issues. Although there are sectors who focus on financial concerns (such as those in the pension, benefit, and insurance sector or the funders and granting organizations sector), they clearly draw on few literary resources to inform the care they provide.

Spirituality and how it might affect one's ministry is another topic we explored in our review of the literatures. By spirituality, we mean the practices that a person might engage in to connect with God or further an individual's discipleship. Slightly more than one in four (27 percent) of our participants' literature discuss spirituality, while only 18 percent of the scholarly literature covers this topic.[11] Some examples from both literatures include *Spiritual Practices for Effective Leadership* and *Spiritual Wholeness for Clergy: A New Psychology of Intimacy with God, Self, and Others*.[12] The scholarly literature mostly focuses on how spirituality could help alleviate burnout or other stresses related to ministry.

Lastly, since many of our participants provide coaching and counseling services to clergy, we were interested in how much of the literature from both sets of sources discusses coaching as a topic. Our research found only 2 percent of the participants' literature and 5 percent of the scholarly

11. We included those resources where the focus was improving one's spiritual health and well-being.

12. Jackson, *Spiritual Practices*; Hands and Fehr, *Spiritual Wholeness*.

literature directly relates to coaching. Despite many of our participants having coaching certifications, they cite very few literary sources that directly inspire and inform their work. The scholarly literature we reviewed discusses the benefits of coaching and how to improve it. An example of this type of literature includes *You Can Coach: How to Help Leaders Build Healthy Churches through Coaching*.[13] As coaching continues to increase as a practice to support and care for clergy, we expect more authors will assess and evaluate this service in their writing.

Audiences

Our final goal in examining the literature of our participants and academics was to compare and contrast specific audiences of their respective texts. Ninety-three percent of the scholarly literature and 26 percent of our participants' literature focuses on clergy, pastors, or ministers (see figure 4–4).[14] Only 3 percent of the resources our participants provided were written explicitly for or about women clergy. For example, Stevenson-Moessner and Snorton's *Women Out of Order: Risking Change and Creating Care in a Multicultural World* incorporates various essays written by women sharing their experiences as women clergy and caring for women clergy. Similarly, scholarly literature that spoke directly to the experiences of women clergy totaled only 3 percent. An example includes David Roebuck's "'I Have Done the Best I Could': Opportunities and Limitations for Women Ministers in the Church of God—A Pentecostal Denomination."

Another audience we considered is communities of color. These texts include any source written specifically for or about communities of color. For participants, 11 percent of their literature speaks to the experiences of communities of color.[15] For example, our participants mentioned Howard Thurman's *Jesus and the Disinherited*, which discusses nonviolent resistance

---

13. Comiskey, *You Can Coach.*

14. Since our methodology meant that we searched exclusively for literature that included the terms clergy, pastor, or minister, most of the academic literature (93 percent) specifically addressed clergy, pastors, and ministers. Those that did not address clergy specifically, focused on religious professionals in general or included clergy as a subsample of the research. This includes all resources that specifically address clergy, pastors, or ministers. A resource discussing the church would not qualify. Some academic examples that focus on clergy include *The Heart of a Great Pastor* and *The Contemplative Pastor.*

15. A resource was included in this category if it specifically addressed issues of concern for communities of color.

and was an inspiration for Rev. Martin Luther King Jr. and other civil rights activists. For academics, less than 5 percent of the literature we reviewed speaks specifically to the experiences of communities of color.

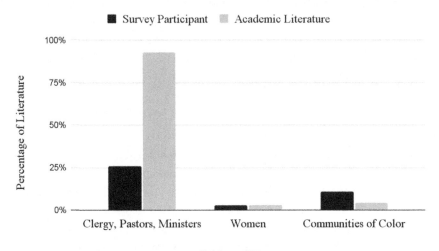

Figure 4–4: Audiences

It is concerning that more texts written specifically for or about women clergy and communities of color have not been published. For these two audiences, there are fewer resources to draw on to inform how clergy care providers address the challenges of their ministry contexts. This is not only a problem for these two audiences but also for clergy overall. Seventy four percent of the literature cited by our participants is not specifically written for or about clergy. Instead, clergy care providers rely on general leadership, nonprofit management, and self-care principles to inform their work. If the literature codifies the field's priorities and values, then the disparities that exist in the texts participants draw on suggest that they are much less able to prioritize the unique needs and concerns of women and communities of color, as well as clergy in general. This finding may be due to unawareness of existing literature rather than the absence of it.

Conclusion

Our decision to review both the academic literature informing the field of clergy care as well as the sources that our participants cite as influential to their work illuminated one of the key points of disconnection within the network of clergy care providers: the literature they consume. Unfortunately, it is clear that the literature our participants consume varies significantly from currently available scholarly literature on clergy care. This incongruence influences how clergy care providers understand the care they provide and the needs of those they serve. Our participants want literature that informs their understanding of healthy clergy who lead healthy congregations. Consequently, they draw on a variety of practical books on leadership and spirituality. On the other hand, the academic literature employs a more psychological framework to understand clergy as a profession susceptible to high rates of burnout. Some academics do care about the sociological factors that shape clergy health and clergy support, but primarily, they explain how individual-level factors such as depression or job satisfaction affect rates of clergy burnout.

The focus on burnout among academics has significant implications for the support of clergy during challenging times. However, these findings may have minimal impact outside of scholarly conversations unless they are translated for and embraced by providers who offer care. Similarly, scholarly inquiry can become dislocated from practical needs and important concerns, without engaging the experiences, struggles, and hopes of clergy and their supporters. The academic community is well-positioned to offer data and analysis on topics such as conflict and polarization or trauma-informed care.[16]

We celebrate the diversity of authors, topics, and themes represented in both the scholarly literature as well as our participant's sources. Each offers a unique perspective that advances our knowledge and understanding of clergy care. Yet, there are significant gaps that need to be addressed. Clergy of color and women clergy are underrepresented in the literature we examined. Few resources exist on topics of concern for clergy in recent years—such as conflict and polarization or trauma. This may be due to the standard lag in the publication process but also suggests the clergy care network must be more responsive to emerging needs. If the field can listen to the needs of clergy and respond more quickly, then providers will be better equipped, and clergy (and their congregations) will receive the support they need.

16. For example, see "Becoming a Trauma-Informed Community" and "Building and Sustaining Relationships in the Midst of Polarization Part I and Part II" at https://commontable.network/.

Clergy care providers often rely on generic materials, not specifically tailored to clergy, their experiences, or their struggles. We support learning from other professions, the nonprofit sector, and general self-care resources. However, these titles address multiple audiences and do not specifically focus on clergy or their challenges in ministry. More concerning, most of the sources cited by our participants are not explicitly Christian and do not touch on concerns of the church.

There is little convergence between the academic and participant's literatures. Simply put, clergy care providers are not reading the same things. These disconnected literatures reinforce silos and hinder effectiveness. As both academics and providers continue to conduct research and publish articles and books, we hope that the findings, approaches, and themes from academic and provider sources can mutually inform each other. When empirical research, theological reflection, and practical grounding create a virtuous cycle, theory becomes more relevant and practical suggestions lead to greater effectiveness. To this end, we encourage scholars to publish in more accessible outlets designed for general audiences including clergy, clergy care providers, and lay leaders. The network of clergy supporters needs research-informed tangible guidelines and practical frameworks.

5

We Aren't Speaking the Same Language

JUST AS THE AVAILABILITY of literature to address the unique needs of a target audience enables clergy care providers to offer focused quality care, the choice of words used by providers matters. Words carry weight that influences, informs, and persuades our thinking. Words have the power to strengthen an organization's ability to operate effectively around a common goal or rally a disparate group of individuals to champion a shared cause. Conversely, when words are not clearly defined or chosen purposefully, an organization's ability to be successful is much less likely, just as the cause of an ambiguous campaign is unlikely to gain momentum.

In the aftermath of the earthquake in Haiti, differing definitions regarding the task at hand caused confusion among the NGOs and impeded their ability to be successful. The problems on the ground were not clearly defined, nor were the solutions. In the void, each NGO determined for itself the core issues and optimal solutions. The lack of clarity invited chaos.

Similarly, although each sector of clergy care providers cares deeply about clergy and their well-being, the network does not have a clear consensus on what clergy well-being means or the root causes that contribute to well-being. Fewer than half of the providers with whom we engaged have a formal definition of clergy well-being, and even when they do have a definition, many do not know what that definition is, the definition is outdated, or the definition is inaccessible. Even the terms that providers use to describe well-being do not always have the same meaning.

Similar to the uncoordinated efforts of care organizations in Haiti, a lack of shared definitions, common terms, and understanding of root problems within the clergy care network creates barriers to collaboration, splinter efforts, and ultimately inhibit clergy from receiving the support they need. In this chapter, we take a deep dive into how the sectors of clergy care providers diverge in their understandings of what defines clergy well-being and the root causes that inform the needs clergy have.

Definitions of Clergy Well-Being[1]

How clergy care providers understand well-being shapes both their understanding of clergy and their response to clergy needs. The words and definitions they use reveal how they reflect on their work and the goals they are working toward. Yet, almost 60 percent of clergy caregivers do not have a formal definition of clergy well-being. When used strategically, a formal definition of clergy well-being influences organizational dynamics. Care providers with a formal definition of clergy well-being are twice as likely to have formal goals for the programs and services they provide for clergy compared to those without a formal definition.[2] As NGOs lacked a vision for a post-earthquake Haiti, most clergy caregivers cannot define what they are trying to achieve or how they are positioned to address targeted areas of need.

Researchers and practitioners draw on a wide range of concepts to inform their understanding of clergy well-being. For example, Matt Bloom, a leading scholar of clergy well-being, says there are four dimensions to well-being: (1) daily well-being, (2) resilience, (3) authenticity, and (4) thriving. However, Wespath Benefits and Investments includes five dimensions of well-being: (1) physical, (2) social, (3) financial, (4) emotional, and

1. In this chapter, our argument concerns how the various conceptualizations of clergy well-being and lack of shared understanding hamper collaboration. We do not argue that there ought to be only one definition of clergy well-being.

2. We used logistic regression analysis in this chapter. A connection also exists between the types of programs and services that organizations provide and the likelihood that they have a formal definition of clergy well-being. Organizations and practices that offer coaching are twice as likely to have a formal definition of well-being compared to those that do not. And those that create support systems (i.e., a structure for a denomination or association to check in on the clergyperson) for the clergyperson are three times more likely to have a formal definition of well-being compared to those that do not. This is likely due to the fact that those who care for the clergyperson's mental health (such as counseling practices) are also more likely to have a formal definition of well-being and provide structure for support systems for clergy.

(5) spiritual. Duke Divinity School's Clergy Health Initiative defines health as "wholeness of body, mind, and spirit."[3]

Given the diversity among the types of clergy care providers, we are not surprised by the wide variety of definitions that exist for clergy well-being. The way a pension, benefit, and insurance official approaches clergy well-being may be distinct from a marriage and family therapist. We find that even when providers from different sectors use the same term, it can have very different meanings. For example, some of our participants associate "holistic" with caring for the mind, body, and spirit. For others, holistic refers to physical, emotional, and spiritual health. Again, others indicate that holistic includes relational and financial concerns. While the first two examples have some overlap, the third is fully distinct.

Multiple definitions of a single term not only apply to concepts of well-being but also to the term "clergy" in general. There is a lack of consensus in the church around what defines the *role* of clergy. John R. Stott writes, "One feature of the contemporary church is its uncertainty about the role of its professional ministers. Are pastors primarily social workers, psychiatrists, educators, facilitators, administrators, or what?"[4] This wide range of professional responsibilities only adds to the challenge of understanding clergy well-being. Without agreed-upon terms or goals, our participants have different ideas as to what constitutes a healthy clergyperson. Definitional variations impede organizations from working together, overcoming silos, and engaging in effective collaboration across sectors.

Of course, a formal definition of clergy well-being is only helpful when the definition is both known and used by members of an organization. Even when an organization formally defines clergy well-being, staff may not know about it. Some participants who cite they have a definition of clergy well-being note that their definition was "difficult to find" or that "the definition needed to be updated."

Concepts of Well-Being

To help the network of clergy caregivers articulate a conceptual framework of clergy well-being, we asked each of our participants—regardless of

3. Bloom, *Flourishing in Ministry;* Duke Global Health Institute, "Duke Clergy Health Initiative"; Wespath Benefits and Investments, *Dimensions.* For another example, see also Howard, *At Full Strength,* 277–95.

4. Stott, "Ideals of Pastoral Ministry," 67.

whether they already had a formal definition of clergy well-being—about the concepts they value and believe should be included in a definition of clergy well-being. We categorized their responses.[5] The following table summarizes our results. The rows sort major concepts by personal well-being and professional well-being. The columns group major concepts by individual well-being and relational well-being.

Concepts of Clergy Well-Being

	Personal Well-Being	Professional Well-Being
Individual Well-Being	Individual Health (Spiritual, Physical, Emotional, Mental)	Professional Health (Learning, Identity, Financial, Rest, Resilience)
Relational Well-Being	Personal-Relational Health (Boundaries, Quality of Relationships)	Professional-Relational Health (Work/Life Balance, Leadership, Support, Community)

In the individual/personal well-being quadrant, our participants focused on individual health, including spiritual, physical, emotional, and mental health. Spiritual health includes responses about the clergyperson's relationship with God and practicing regular spiritual disciplines. Physical health includes regular exercise and activity. Emotional and mental health refers to a clergyperson's ability to share and express emotions and the absence or prevention of depression, stress, and anxiety.

In the relational/personal well-being quadrant, our participants noted the importance of healthy boundaries, a concept that appeared throughout our research. Two denominational officials noted that setting boundaries provides parameters that protect a clergyperson's individual well-being as well as their family and their relationship with God.

The individual/professional well-being quadrant includes terms that address how clergy engage in ministry. For some of our participants, this means lifelong learning and engaging in scholarly pursuits throughout one's career. Our participants noted resilience as it relates to how well clergy are able to navigate the challenges and hardships of ministry. Similarly, the concept of identity was also included in this category so that, as one

---

5. We coded these responses to identify the concepts important to our participants. We then grouped the concepts in a table to show how they relate to each other. Some of these concepts can overlap the quadrants. For instance, we could argue that boundaries have a place in each quadrant.

participant noted, the clergyperson has a "clear sense of identity in their context." This concept was important for the clergy of color we interviewed because they said care should be culturally appropriate. As one of our participants noted, sometimes clergy need "healing from the traumas of racism, sexism, homophobia, xenophobia, and other forms of hate." Many participants expressed the importance of concepts like work-life balance and practicing Sabbath. Participants often cited financial health because it references the clergyperson's ability to manage both personal and congregational finances.

Lastly, the relational/professional well-being quadrant focuses on relationships and networks. Some of our participants believe boundaries help clergy develop healthy personal relationships and manage their congregations' demands. Many participants think that possessing particular leadership qualities (such as servant leadership, collaboration, adaptability) can help clergy become healthier leaders for their congregations and communities. Finally, the concept of support refers to clergy having people in their lives on whom they can rely such as peers, friends, or caregivers.

We do not want to convey that our participants generally conceptualize clergy well-being in ways that fit neatly in a two-by-two matrix. Most participants emphasize only a few concepts scattered among the four quadrants. In fact, we find that many participants include only individual/personal concepts while others only include professional/relational concepts. Individual/personal concepts constitute 50 percent of the participants' total responses. Of these, spiritual health appeared far more frequently than any other concept in this quadrant. Spiritual health appears more than twice as often as mental health. Therefore, it appears the network of providers caring for clergy tends to understand clergy well-being as mostly individual and spiritual.

In a series of focus groups we conducted on the concepts of clergy well-being, we noticed that more racially diverse groups were more likely to discuss clergy well-being from the standpoint of the community than the individual. In these instances, "clergy well-being" does not exist apart from communal and relational well-being. This interconnected understanding of clergy health shows the importance of relationships and context—especially since the vast majority of the scholarly literature on clergy well-being is written from the standpoint of the individual and their personal well-being. Overall, these focus groups highlighted how the field of clergy care might benefit from adopting a broader concept of clergy well-being.

Concepts by Sector

We sorted the responses on clergy well-being by each sector to identify how the five clergy care sectors differed in their definition of clergy well-being. As figure 5–1 shows, each of the five sectors has different priorities.[6] Pension, benefit, and insurance providers and grantors and funders tend to see financial well-being as critical for overall clergy well-being. In contrast, continuing educators are much less likely to include financial well-being as an aspect of clergy well-being. We find that continuing educators and frontline providers understand clergy well-being as primarily a spiritual matter. In addition to the work they do in the classroom, continuing educators often provide pastoral care and counseling. One-fourth of the responses continuing educators gave addressed spiritual health.[7]

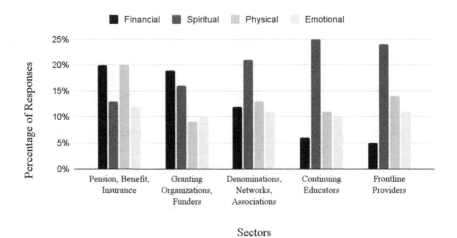

Figure 5–1: Sectors and Top Four Well-Being Concepts

The denominations, networks, and associations sector differs from the other sectors in that those within this sector are a third less likely to have a *formal* definition of clergy well-being.[8] Denominations, networks, and as-

6. Figure 5–1 shows only our participants' top four concepts related to clergy well-being—physical, financial, spiritual, and mental/emotional health.

7. This is slightly more than that of the full sample (21 percent). Compared to the rest of the network, continuing educators are more likely to define clergy well-being as spiritual rather than using other terms such as financial.

8. Regardless of whether they have a formal definition or not, the denomination, network, and association sector participants all had ideas about the concepts associated

sociations have many different interests in helping clergy.[9] For instance, one of our participants discussed how her denomination was hoping to prevent clergy attrition by providing financial support for clergy to get away for two weeks and rest. Other participants who work with denominations or networks also help clergy manage financial resources, both their own and their congregation's. Notably, in contrast to the continuing educators, few in this sector see clergy well-being as primarily a spiritual matter.

The denominations, networks, and associations sector's relative lack of attention to spiritual health could be due to competing priorities with other concepts related to well-being such as financial responsibility and emotional health. This is a diverse sector with many varying interests in supporting clergy. Although our interviewees often claimed that they were committed to developing leadership skills, creating work-life balance, and providing supportive groups for the clergy they serve, each of these concepts appeared in fewer than 5 percent of the responses (hence the reason they are not shown in the figure). Our participants might value these concepts in a definition of clergy well-being, but denominations, networks, and associations (and the other sectors) prioritize them much less compared to values related to spiritual, physical, financial, and mental/emotional health.

The frontline providers resemble the previous two sectors; however, they are more likely to define clergy well-being in terms of their mental/emotional health. For example, one frontline provider said that well-being entailed emotional awareness. Another provider added that clergy well-being required emotionally healthy individuals, families, and marriages.

The remaining two sectors stand out in their divergence from the priorities of the rest of the network. Both funders/granting organizations and pension, benefits, and insurance providers highly prioritize financial wellness as a key concept that defines clergy well-being. Lately, concerns of financial well-being have shaped funders' priorities given fluctuations in the economy and data suggesting that more clergy are bivocational or

---

with clergy well-being.

9. The denomination, network, and association sector is slightly more likely (60 percent) than our full sample of participants to include health-related concepts as important indicators of well-being. They are also slightly less likely to include relational concepts as important for well-being (17 percent). Nearly one in four responses from continuing educators and frontline providers prioritized spiritual health as key in a definition of clergy well-being; however, the proportion was closer to one in five for the denominations, networks, and associations sector.

part-time due to fewer churches able to support full-time clergy.[10] For example, many of our participants have participated in grant initiatives such as the Lilly Endowment's Thriving in Ministry or Economic Challenges Facing Pastoral Leaders.[11] The Thriving in Ministry initiative includes a focus on clergy financial well-being particularly during times of transition such as retirement.

There is also growing interest among our participants in how financial challenges might impact women clergy and clergy of color when compared to white male clergy. One participant desired culturally appropriate care that is affordable and support for clergy when they face challenges due to the current socio-cultural environment. Half of the responses related to "support" referenced providing for the financial well-being of clergy so that the clergy could also enjoy the support of family, friends, other clergy, and the community. As the United States continues to grapple with racism and other forms of discrimination, we expect clergy care providers to define well-being in terms of support from the community and equal access to care.

Figure 5–1 does not show relational concepts because they did not appear in any of the sectors' top four concepts of clergy well-being. Each sector was more likely to define clergy well-being using individual/personal concepts than relational ones. This indicates that clergy care providers tend to view the clergyperson and their well-being in isolation rather than in the context of their community.

Only slightly more than 40 percent of our participants work for an organization with a formal definition of clergy well-being, and many more do not know what the definition is, even if their organization has one. Regardless of whether or not our participants have a formal definition, there is a great variety in the concepts the participants believe are important for defining clergy well-being. This not only makes it more difficult to collaborate with others in caring for clergy but also means that clergy themselves encounter a variety of ideas as to what it means for them to be well.

If a clergyperson sees a therapist regularly, connects with their denomination monthly, receives health insurance from a pension/benefit provider, and is enrolled in a doctor of ministry course, they implicitly or explicitly encounter providers who understand clergy well-being differently. Helping the field understand how clergy well-being is defined could

10. National Congregations Study, "National Survey of Religious Leaders."

11. See https://thrivinginministry.org/.

improve the facilitation of conversation between parties, offer the opportunity for greater collaboration, and ultimately lead to more effectiveness in the care provided to clergy.

Our goal in sharing figure 5–1 is for each sector to understand how the other sectors prioritize various aspects of clergy well-being. We hope that understanding can make conversations and collaboration among the different sectors easier and ultimately beneficial for the clergyperson. Each sector does not have to exactly resemble the others in how it conceptualizes clergy well-being. Diversity is good and reflects the various goals and experiences among the sectors. However, just as an organization's mission statement helps clarify the organization's values, so too knowing the priorities of each sector helps the sectors to complement each other as they collaborate to improve the programs and services they offer to clergy.

Root Causes

In our survey we asked participants to list programs and services they provide to care for clergy. We then asked them to specify the problems that those programs and services address. In most cases, our participants understood these root causes as threats to clergy well-being. We coded these responses to better understand problems and root causes our participants identified.[12] The results broadly map onto the concepts of well-being mentioned earlier.

How Participants Understand Root Causes

	Personal Root Causes	Professional Root Causes
Individual Root Causes	Spiritual health	Burnout
	Trauma	Busyness
	Lack of self-awareness	Efficacy
	Mental health	Finances
	Unhealthy behaviors	Lack of education
Relational Root Causes	Leadership and growth	Unhealthy church
		Congregational demands

12. Participants may believe that there are other root issues to address in caring for clergy, but they have prioritized the above for their programs. Similar to the well-being table, some of these concepts can overlap the quadrants. For instance, we could argue that burnout is also a personal root cause. The main point is to understand the four quadrants, not to qualify each of the items in each of the quadrants.

In the individual/personal quadrant, participants noted problems that are associated with the individual. Nearly half of our participants referred to spiritual health as the problem they are trying to solve. Spiritual health includes spiritual formation, discipleship, and a close, personal relationship with God. Participants also see issues related to trauma as an underlying root cause. Our participants associate trauma with problems related to a clergyperson's family of origin and, at times, their ministry. Lack of self-awareness refers to the clergyperson's inability to understand their own stress or other challenges. Some of our participants want to help clergy become more aware of who they are as clergy and the struggles they may be denying to themselves. Self-awareness could also entail a greater sense of one's strengths and gifts. Quite a few participants highlighted mental health as foundational to the overall health of clergy. Some participants included unhealthy behaviors (i.e., addiction and poor coping mechanisms) as the root cause of clergy health.

Root causes that fell into the individual/professional quadrant were the most frequently cited by our participants overall. This quadrant deals with the problems clergy face in their ministry. According to our participants, the root cause of poor well-being is often the professional challenges clergy face. Clergy caregivers see the demands and expectations of ministry as significant concerns that can lead to burnout and busyness. The need to experience effectiveness in one's ministry as a root cause was one we saw in both the survey and interviews.[13] Some of our participants believed that when clergy do not feel effective, they are more likely to leave ministry. Participants more frequently cited financial issues as a root cause than any other concept. Since two sectors emphasize the financial dimension of clergy well-being (funders and granting organizations and pension, benefit, and insurance organizations), we would expect to see a similar focus on finances as a root cause of clergy well-being.

The relational/personal and relational/professional quadrants only included two concepts—leadership and growth and unhealthy church. However, these two concepts amounted to a significant proportion (15 percent) of participants' responses to the root causes they address. Our participants recognize that leadership skills are essential to performing the role of a clergyperson, but many clergy do not naturally possess the qualities and

---

13. Effectiveness in one's ministry refers to the clergyperson's ability to believe that they are doing well in their work and accomplishing their work-related goals. Some of our participants referred to this concept as "efficacy."

skills of a healthy leader without the support of clergy care providers. Our participants identify the need for growth in leadership skills as key to the clergyperson's health and well-being. The concept of unhealthy church refers to how unhealthy dynamics in the community led by the clergyperson can affect their well-being. Collaboration among churches, organizational practices and culture, conflict and polarization, forced termination, and transitions of church leadership are all examples of root causes that are relational/professional.

Terms in the relational row are the least frequently cited as both concepts of well-being and root causes. Although relationships impact issues of leadership and the clergyperson's health, participants to our survey do not often cite relationships as a leading root cause. Our results suggest that providers tend to see, understand, and treat clergy in isolation.

In select cases (only 2 percent), our participants cited preventative measures that do not map neatly onto the matrix above. One participant said that their organization focuses on prevention in order to be more proactive about pastoral resignations. This individual observed resignations among pastors and decided to implement a mentorship program where a senior pastor mentored a young pastor for three years. This program helped to reduce the rate of pastors resigning from ministry and hoped to prevent burnout and isolation.

Each of the quadrants address issues that are relevant to many clergy but might exclude others. For example, many participants focused on the needs of married clergy; however, our participants rarely attended to the needs of single clergy. Additionally, in our interviews with our participants when they say they help clergy handle the demands and expectations of their congregation, our participants may assume they are helping senior leaders and not leaders in less prominent roles such as worship leader or children's pastor.

Root Causes by Sector

Each sector has its own particular understanding of the root causes it needs to address in order to care for clergy. The following sector-specific analysis identifies how the sectors differ in their understanding of the root causes of poor health among clergy. For collaboration among the sectors to occur, it is important for each to understand the differing conceptualization of the causes of clergy well-being that they are focused on addressing in the care they provide.

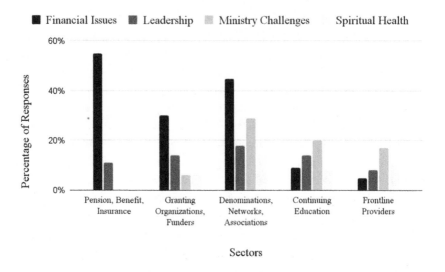

Figure 5–2: Sectors and Root Causes

Figure 5–2 shows the top four concepts related to root causes for each sector. The results indicate even more disconnect between the sectors on the root causes than we saw in the concepts of well-being. Similar to the concepts of well-being, the pension, benefit, and insurance sector and the granting organizations and funders sector view the root causes of clergy in terms of financial issues. More than 40 percent of the responses from denominations, networks, and associations participants specify financial issues as a root cause. However, only 10 percent of them define well-being using financial concepts. This sector identifies the role that financial issues play as a root cause of clergy health, but that does not mean they include financial wellness as critical for clergy well-being.

Continuing Educators

Continuing educators see ministry challenges as one of the main root causes that they are addressing. Spiritual health is less than 10 percent of the responses and relationship issues is just over 5 percent of the responses related to root causes. Most of the root causes continuing educators addressed are only a fraction of the sector's total responses because the sector addresses a diverse range of root causes. Though the sector itself is mostly composed of seminary professors, other academics, and continuing education providers affiliated with other organizations, they manage to be quite diversified in the root causes they address.

Denominations, Networks, and Associations

In contrast to continuing educators, the denominations, networks, and associations sector is more likely to name financial issues as the root cause that they are addressing in their care for clergy. Nearly 50 percent of their responses address financial issues as a root cause. For continuing education providers, only 10 percent of their responses address financial issues.

We see the denomination, network, and association sector's top root causes (financial and ministry) as consistent with what we would expect given their role in caring for clergy. The two root causes (not shown in figure 5–2) that fall surprisingly low on the list are relationship issues and an unhealthy church. We would expect that denominations that are concerned with the overall health of their denomination would be more concerned about the effect of unhealthy churches on the well-being of their clergy. Similarly, we heard consistently from our interviewees that clergy are lonely and isolated. However, loneliness and isolation do not prominently factor as root causes addressed by the denominations, networks, and associations sector. It seems as though this sector (and others) leave the focus on relationships to the care and attention of frontline providers.

Another notable absence from the responses is any discussion of trauma. Even as research establishes the impact of trauma on a variety of outcomes,[14] we do not find that any participants from the denominations, networks, or associations sector address trauma as a root cause. As we saw in chapter 4, even if academics research trauma, that does not necessarily mean that participants are accessing that research. As more and more research establishes the impact of trauma on a variety of outcomes, it is surprising that few participants from the sectors address trauma as a root cause. Despite the discussion of trauma by our interviewees and the increasing interest in how it shapes clergy well-being, few participants—especially participants from the denominations, networks, and associations sector who play a critical role throughout a clergyperson's career—regularly

14. See Hendron et al., "Unseen Cost."

draw on resources that inform their understanding of trauma. They also do not see trauma as a root cause of clergy health and well-being.

Frontline Providers

Although frontline providers cite mental health in only 10 percent of their responses, they mention mental health more frequently as a root cause than continuing educators or those from denominations, networks, and associations. Many frontline providers such as counselors, marriage and family therapists, and coaches by nature of their profession are more attuned to how mental health affects the well-being of clergy.

As noted above, frontline providers included spiritual health in nearly 25 percent of their responses to the concepts and values they believed important in a definition of well-being and as a need that they address. However, even though spiritual health was the most important factor shaping clergy well-being according to frontline providers, they are more likely to focus on ministry challenges as the root cause of clergy health that needs to be addressed. We find this surprising, especially given the number of therapists and counselors who are frontline providers. Even though they are more likely than other sectors to identify mental health related causes of clergy health, they see ministry challenges as the top factor affecting clergy well-being. The sectors' agreement on ministry challenges as a root cause can create points of connection to collaborate with other sectors in addressing the ministry-related challenges.

Granting Organizations and Funders

Far more than any other factor, financial issues are the root cause that granting organizations and funders address. This sector addresses a variety of other root causes, but most of those root causes do not constitute more than 7 percent of their responses. This singular focus on financial issues poses a challenge for this sector and the network of clergy caregivers. If each sector has its own interpretation of the root cause of clergy ill health, then it will be difficult for the sectors to find common ground to work on addressing clergy health and well-being. The granting organizations and funders sector can identify other root causes as critical to clergy well-being, even though it is not a need that they address. This overriding focus becomes even more apparent in our findings from the pension, benefit, and insurance sector.

Pension, Benefit, and Insurance Providers

Nearly 60 percent of the responses from the pension, benefit, and insurance sector named financial issues as a root cause that they address. That rate is nearly double that of granting organizations and funders. Ministry challenges did not even appear despite their significance for other sectors. Figure 5–2 also indicates that the pension, benefit, and insurance sector is somewhat limited in its interpretation of the root causes of health in clergy. This singular perspective poses a challenge to their ability to collaborate with other sectors. It is not just that they have differing emphases, but the pension, benefit, and insurance sector does not report the root causes upon which other sectors focus.

Just as we saw in the section on well-being, the field of clergy care providers does not have a clear consensus on the root causes of clergy health that it addresses. The existence of silos among the different sectors affects the field's ability to align on a shared understanding of root causes. As we saw in Haiti, the lack of shared understanding of the root causes leads to further disorganization of the care provided.

Conclusion

In this chapter, we addressed how each sector conceptualizes clergy well-being and the root causes of this well-being. The way providers define well-being reflects their values and priorities. We also find that the way this network understands clergy well-being influences its understanding of root causes. The next chapter will address how these concepts and root causes affect the needs each sector chooses to address.

Our findings lead us to conclude that understanding and formalizing clergy well-being and its causes may have practical implications for the type of programs and services offered within the field. With that said, we do not think there needs to be a single definition of clergy well-being. Rather, we advocate for a shared understanding of core concepts and values. Consider theologians, anthropologists, and psychologists. They all have differing understandings of human nature due to the different literatures that inform their disciplines. However, when they meet to collaborate and learn from each other, their unique disciplines are complementary. Although they may contribute varying insights from their unique disciplines, they are able to grasp how the others in the room approach and view human nature because they have an understanding of each other's core concepts and values. We believe the same complementary relationship between sectors in regard to clergy well-being and root causes is more realistic for the network than a single definition.

After the 2010 earthquake in Haiti, donors channeled billions of dollars through NGOs to help the country restore its infrastructure. More than a decade later, Haiti is still just as vulnerable to natural disasters.[15] The NGOs lacked a shared understanding of the root issues at hand and what success meant for the Haitian people. There could be a similar outcome for clergy if the sectors do not learn how each one varies in its understanding of clergy well-being and the root causes at play. If the sectors can reach a shared understanding, they have the ability to be more effective in collaborating and improving the programs and services they provide for clergy.

15. Douyon and Sepinwall, "Earthquakes and Storms."

6

What Are We Providing?

SETH WALKER ONCE SERVED as an evangelical pastor.[1] Over the course of his career, he ministered faithfully to drug addicts, domestic abusers (and their victims), the poor, and those committing self-harm. He was respected by his staff and loved by his parishioners. Unfortunately, today, Seth considers himself an atheist.

Seth's departure from both his ministry and faith happened slowly. While his congregation required increasing levels of investment from him, he felt more and more alone. He was burning out, one exhausting church event after another. His mental health waned, and soon, so did his faith. He attempted suicide. He questioned his calling; he questioned God. Without a support network to fall back on as the very foundation of his life began to crack, he left the church.

Seth's personal journey with God and his own struggle with mental health is complex, but one thing is certain: the severity of his struggles within ministry were heightened by the reality that he faced them alone. At the very least, that reality should be preventable—for Seth and countless others like him. Seth needed support both professionally and personally, yet he felt he had access to neither. How might Seth's story have differed if there had been people readily positioned to care for him along the way?

1. The following account is adapted from the memoir of Seth Walker. For more information, see Walker, *Faithless*; Goswami, "How Did Gifted Christian."

L. Gregory Jones once said that an honest advertisement for pastoral ministry might read: "Manage conflict and slow decline for long hours and little pay." Certainly, the demands of ministry can be overwhelming, and the toil of ministry impacts clergy well-being.[2] In 2010, Rae Jean Proeschold-Bell and Sara LeGrand found that clergy's physical health fared worse than the general population by measures of obesity, diabetes, arthritis, and hypertension.[3] In 2014, Meghan Baruth, Sara Wilcox, and Rebecca Evans showed this disparity to be especially true in pastoral communities of color due to multiple and extreme stressors.[4] In 2017, Matt Bloom found that more than a third of interviewed pastors reported high-to-severe levels of burnout.[5] In 2019, following a series of high-profile pastoral suicides, the Billy Graham Center hosted a gathering to discuss an emerging mental health crisis among pastors.[6]

The strain of the COVID-19 pandemic has also taken its toll. Separated from their congregations during lockdown, many pastors felt isolated and alone. The pandemic exacerbated fatigue, weariness, and stress. Tired of fighting partisan battles and members more concerned with protecting their political interests than the mission of the church, some clergy have contemplated a change in their career. As one pastor, fed up with his congregants' conspiracy theories, recently said, "I don't need this anymore," after one of the church members called him the antichrist.

What Do Clergy Need?[7]

Broadly speaking, we discovered that the needs our participants have identified in the lives of the clergy they serve can be divided into three major categories: professional needs, health needs, and relational needs.[8] Figure

2. Carroll, *God's Potters*, 159–87.

3. Proeschold-Bell and LeGrand, "High Rates of Obesity."

4. Baruth et al., "Health and Health Behaviors," 229.

5. Bloom, "Burning Out in Ministry."

6. Morrison, "Wheaton Summit."

7. This section draws on the clergy caregiver's perspective of what clergy need. We make no claims as to if these needs are what clergy would identify, but understanding the perceived needs of providers is helpful and informative.

8. Our survey asked our participants to identify the needs they see among clergy. We provided our participants with a list of needs to choose from. Each participant could select multiple needs that their organization addressed. Consequently, the needs we discuss are based on our original assumptions about the needs the field of clergy caregivers

6–1 indicates the distribution of each of these broad categories and the specific needs that contribute to each of its component parts.

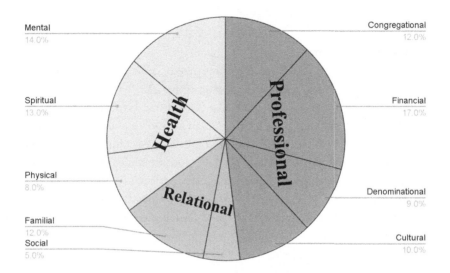

Figure 6–1: Identified Needs

Professional Needs

Nearly half (48 percent) of the needs our participants have identified relate to a clergyperson's ministerial profession. According to our interviewees, professional needs serve as the primary motivation for clergy to seek help. However, the exploration of professional needs often reveals deeper issues related to health concerns (e.g., anxiety, depression) or relational needs (e.g., marital trouble, parenting challenges).

Professionally, clergy face challenges associated with their congregations, denominations, culture at-large and find themselves in need of support. At the local (congregational) level, our participants often identify needs related to conflict within congregations. These needs include dealing with critical church members, staff conflict, and congregation members with unrealistic expectations.

---

addressed. As we will see in the following chapter, the results of our coding of well-being concepts and root concepts suggest that other needs might be addressed such as community, efficacy in ministry, and leadership skills.

At the denominational level, those caring for clergy identify needs associated with transitional moments such as ordination, changing congregations, and retirement. Each of these transitions is a key moment in the clergyperson's career that can affect their well-being. Some providers work exclusively within a single denominational tradition, while others work across many traditions.

Not all clergy will have the same needs during these transitions, however. For instance, the needs of bivocational clergy vary from those in full-time ministry. One participant, Andy, said that bivocational ministry is seen as the "stepchild" of full-time ministry. Unfortunately, given the historical status of bivocational ministry, it has been easy for denominations and other sectors to overlook the needs (and schedules) of bivocational clergy. According to several participants, only recently have theological institutions begun to seriously consider the preparation of bivocational leaders for the twenty-first century, even though bivocational ministry has long been practiced. Approximately 73 percent of the clergy care providers in our research provide programs or services for bivocational clergy.

From a cultural standpoint, our participants identified professional challenges associated with ministering in an increasingly secular society.[9] For instance, many clergy confront hot-button topics such as racism, sexism, and political polarization in their ministry. Consider the impact of the Black Lives Matter movement, the Me Too and Church Too movements, and recent presidential elections, as well as COVID-19 mask and vaccine mandates. We find that clergy often need support from providers to effectively minister to their congregations in the midst of these cultural challenges. Clergy struggle to rest, often feeling pressure to be "on" at all times with little, if any, time off.

Additionally, cultural needs can often involve addressing gender roles and expectations within the church. Andrea, a continuing education provider, shared that instructors in her seminary often describe the experience of ministry from the perspective of a man. Women clergy often experience different challenges and express different forms of leadership than clergymen. Andrea has worked on the inclusion of women's perspectives in the curriculum to highlight the support women clergy need.

---

9. For the first time, Gallup found that Americans' membership in religious institutions had dropped below 50 percent (now at 47 percent) in 2020. Jones, "U.S. Church Membership Falls."

Lastly, clergy need support as they face financial challenges related to financial literacy and financial well-being. We interviewed a financial counselor who said it is often difficult for clergy to share about financial difficulties either at home or in the church. Pastors feel shame if they have not had training to know how to manage personal or church-related finances. The financial counselor said this shame affects how pastors relate to their congregation because clergy often hide the fact that they have not learned the skills of financial management.

Health Needs

Thirty-five percent of the needs our participants have identified are health-related: experiencing challenges with their mental, spiritual, and physical well-being. Concurrently, our participants particularly underscore the importance of addressing mental health needs. In chapter 3, we introduced Ron, who runs a retreat center specializing in clergy recovery programs. He discovered the urgency of addressing health needs when he received the results from a survey of pastors he conducted. Ron was shocked by the number of pastors who reported stress disorders and compassion fatigue and had thought about quitting their jobs. Other participants shared similar stories of their shock when they learned about the degree of stress and anxiety many clergy face.

From a spiritual health perspective, clergy care providers attend to the spiritual practices that they believe will help encourage the clergyperson's faith and help them have a closer relationship with God. These "soul care" practices include a variety of programs from seeking solitude with God to prayer, fasting, spiritual direction, and accountability groups. These and other spiritual disciplines provide essential support for clergy. The absence of spiritual growth leads to harmful effects not only in the clergyperson's relationships but also in his or her ministry.

Providers also express concern for the physical health of clergy. In her coaching practice, Heather implemented an accountability program where clergy log their physical activity and diet. Heather encourages her clients to establish and make progress toward fitness and nutrition goals. She believes that clergy cannot have healthy spiritual lives without also having healthy physical practices.

Relational Needs

Considering the three broad categories of needs, our participants are less likely to identify relational needs than professional and health needs. This is consistent with the previous chapter that showed relational concepts receive less attention than other areas. Although the category of family and marriage occupies 12 percent of total needs,[10] we hypothesize that the relatively small size of this category could be due to how relationships may be addressed in conjunction with other needs and not as the primary focus of a program. For example, many of our interviewees stated that some clergy who struggle with their relationships seek treatment instead for depression. One participant, Rick, said that building healthy relationships is the "long game." Rick might not help pastors with their relationships directly, but he hopes that healthier relationships will emerge as clergy make other healthy changes in their lives. Rick believes that healthy relationships ultimately sustain a clergyperson and keep them well.

We find that the lack of attention to relational needs, while it affects all clergy, can have exacerbated consequences for women clergy. One of the key categories of relational needs entails addressing the needs of the clergyperson's relationship with and their care for their family—a burden that often disproportionately falls on women. The same cultural expectations for a more masculine style of leadership that exclude women from top positions in ministry may make it more difficult for congregations to adequately compensate them for additional financial burdens such as childcare or caring for aging parents. Sociologists Cyrus Schleifer and Amy Miller find that women clergy with children are paid less than women clergy without children.[11] Only 25 percent of our participants provide programs or services to help clergy care for their marriages or families, 8 percent offer services to help clergy care for aging parents, 17 percent help clergy with parenting. To better support women clergy, more programs and services for taking care of families will be needed.

Retreat center hosts we spoke with also maintained that relationships are essential for clergy well-being. However, many retreat centers focus on the personal "inner work" pastors need to do and not the relational challenges clergy face. Certainly, providers hope this inner work will lead to

---

10. The family and marriage category combines responses of caring for marriage, parents, and children.

11. Schleifer and Miller, "Occupational Gender Inequality."

healthier relationships. However, relationships are not the priority of the training. Another popular type of clergy retreat focuses on marital relationships, where clergy spouses participate in the process. Yet, these marriage enrichment seminars and retreats may not address the need clergy (and spouses) have for supportive friendships or care related to relationships within their congregations. Although most clergy are married, a significant percentage are single.[12] However, none of our participants specifically noted that they address the unique relational needs of single clergy.

Clergy may also find it difficult to make and retain supportive relationships or friendships outside of their congregations. Our participants told us that they often hear that clergy do not know who to trust either as friends or for professional help. As a result, clergy tend to be less likely to seek help for fostering healthy relationships.

What Does Each Sector Prioritize?

Variation exists in how likely each sector is to provide programs or services that meet the professional, health, and relational needs of clergy. For example, pension, benefit, and insurance officers and granting organizations and funders stand out from the rest of the field in their prioritization of financial issues. Accordingly, this orientation towards financial concerns impacts the needs these sectors address, increasing the likelihood that organizations in both sectors address the needs of financial literacy and financial well-being.

Many clergy do not receive education on how to manage a nonprofit organization such as a congregation. Even when they do have the right knowledge, they may lack the tools or face unforeseen financial challenges. Everence Financial is a financial services provider that offers services for a number of faith-based individuals and groups. They developed the Pastoral Financial Wellness Program to provide clergy with the tools and support they need to effectively manage their congregation's financial resources.

On the other hand, the prioritization of financial concerns can mean that organizations in the pension, benefit, and insurance sector and the funders and grantors sector are less likely to address other needs of clergy. For instance, both granting organizations and funders are one-third less likely than the rest of the field to attend to mental health needs and half as likely to identify needs related to spiritual health. Pension, benefit,

12. National Congregations Study, "National Survey of Religious Leaders."

and insurance providers are also half as likely to identify needs related to spiritual health. As we saw in the previous chapter, while both sectors cite spiritual health as one of the primary components of clergy well-being,[13] they do not see spiritual health as a root cause that they address. These two sectors do not identify the same root causes as the rest of the field. Accordingly, they leave the care for a clergyperson's spiritual needs to the other sectors. Instead, these two sectors understand clergy well-being primarily from the lens of physical health. As a result, these organizations are four times more likely to provide programs and services that address physical well-being.

Continuing education providers are balanced in their priorities of addressing clergy needs. As an example, Austin Presbyterian Theological Seminary provides a resource for current clergy called the College of Pastoral Leaders. This initiative provides grant money for groups of clergy to design their own program of restoration and renewal. Clergy can use the money for learning opportunities, rest, and to build a community of support with other clergy. They can work on their mental and spiritual health, pursue continuing education and lifelong learning, hone leadership skills, and foster critical community with trusted peers and mentors. In this way, the initiative attends to multiple needs of clergy rather than specifying that the grant money be used for priorities of the seminary itself such as educational or spiritual initiatives.

Similarly, denominations, networks, and associations do not place heavy emphasis on one particular need over another. The Alliance for Greater Works is an example of a network that invests money in caring for church leaders and their communities, addresses trauma and other mental health issues, and supports clergy in their relationship with the sociocultural context. Located in Texas, the Alliance for Greater Works aims to equip Black churches and their leaders across the state. One of their most recent initiatives, the Resilient Church Collective, provides resources for church leaders to address the trauma of their congregants and local community members. Church leaders do not automatically know how to help others process and heal from trauma, especially when the leaders themselves experienced the same or similar traumatic events. This initiative launched by the Alliance for Greater Works provides church leaders with guidance and the resources they need to lead their communities through the process of healing from trauma. Through this initiative, the Alliance for

13. See ch. 5.

Greater Works helps clergy with financial issues, church difficulties, mental health, and community support.

Some denominations, such as the Evangelical Free Church of America, offer recovery programs that place the pastor and his or her family within a new congregation without any formal duties. These programs support clergy while they work through their burnout, trauma, or moral failing. The denomination assists pastors with their housing and financial concerns while they take time away from the church they formerly pastored. The pastors also receive spiritual direction, and the denomination helps the pastor's family adjust to a new environment and establish community. The goal is ultimately to restore the pastor back to a pastoral office. In doing so, they address their financial, spiritual, and relational needs.

We saw in chapter 5 that frontline providers prioritize mental and spiritual health as indicators of clergy well-being. They also identify health needs as a root cause. Accordingly, frontline providers are three times more likely than the full sample to address clergy's mental health needs.[14] Frontline providers are five times more likely than other sectors to care for marital health.[15] We see a pattern emerging between the concepts and root causes the sectors identify. For instance, frontline providers are the most likely to understand clergy well-being from a relational standpoint and see relational needs as the root cause. Consequently, in comparison to the other sectors, they are more likely to address relational needs such as those associated with a clergyperson's marriage.

Concentration of Support

In our surveys, interviews, and focus groups, we asked providers to select from a list of commonly offered types of support within their sector. Figure 6–2 displays the overall results. Clearly, educational opportunities are provided most often. Nearly 75 percent of our participants offer continued education services. Although some types of support such as "spiritual direction" tend to be limited to the frontline provider sector, continuing

14. The exact probability varies by specific profession. Counseling centers are nearly four times more likely to address mental health needs. Retreat centers are five times more likely to care for mental health than other types of organizations.

15. Counseling and retreat centers are six times more likely to care about the clergyperson's aging parents. Counseling centers are twelve times more likely to care about the parenting responsibilities of the clergyperson.

education bridges all the sectors that support clergy. Many seminaries provide continuing education programs, but retreat centers, pension, benefit, and insurance organizations, and denominational bodies do as well. These continuing education seminars relate to everything from financial management and fundraising to pastoral care and counseling.

Clergy value opportunities for continuing education for many reasons. Sometimes they seek out continuing education programs for pragmatic reasons. In these cases, clergy may not feel that their theological education gave them the tools they need for practical ministry. There can be other motivations also. According to our participants, some clergy seek continuing education to run from a problem or to run towards something new. For some, the pursuit of continuing education can mask underlying problems with family, congregations, or themselves. In interviews with doctor of ministry directors, we discovered that many find themselves offering counseling to their students who are either burnt out or barely hanging on in ministry. For others, continuing education can be used as a way to transition from one type of career to another. The classroom offers a "proper" way to exit a local congregation for service in a different setting.

Relatively few of our participants address issues related to conflict resolution, support for racial justice, or diversity training.[16] This finding surprised us, as our survey was distributed a year after the murder of George Floyd and the wave of protests for Black Lives Matter that followed. As we have noted, countless congregations have experienced conflict over sociopolitical issues. However, relatively few providers offer services that address these issues. This finding raises questions concerning how well the field is preparing clergy to respond to sociopolitical and cultural challenges. These concerns are particularly relevant when it comes to meeting the needs of women clergy, bivocational clergy, and clergy of color.

Nearly two-thirds of our participants stated that they were effective in reaching the needs of women and clergy of color. Three-fourths of them provide programs and services for bivocational clergy. Despite this promising assessment of our participants' effectiveness in meeting the needs of women clergy, bivocational clergy, and clergy of color, others in our focus groups and interviews asserted much more is needed to effectively provide for these populations. For example, in a focus group with providers who care

16. Twenty-three percent of our participants offer programs on conflict resolution. Nineteen percent of our participants provide support related to injustice. Twenty-three percent of our participants provide diversity training.

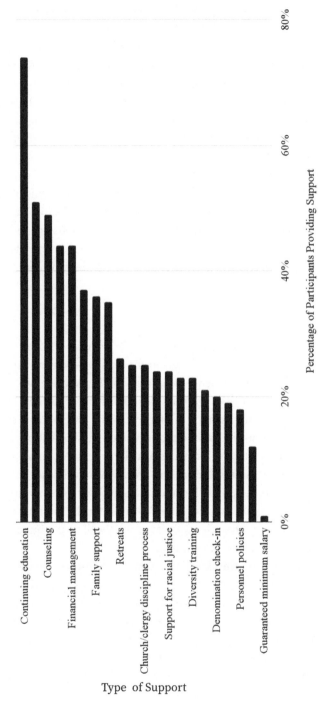

Figure 6–2: Types of Support Provided

for women clergy, our participants stated that there needs to be more investment in spaces that value the leadership of women clergy, which often entails needing additional resources to help women with childcare responsibilities and their responsibilities of caring for aging parents. Yet, very few of our participants currently invest resources providing for these needs.

It is no secret that prioritizing care for women clergy, bivocational clergy, and clergy of color can create conflict or division in some theological traditions. Some clergy care providers may feel ill-equipped to help women clergy, bivocational clergy, and clergy of color navigate the kind of conflict and division evident in our society. Consequently, while our participants noted that clergy have experienced exhaustion from these kinds of cultural divisions in society and within the church, they can more easily care for the burnout or exhaustion clergy experience during these tensions rather than the underlying conflict and division. Thus, there is an ongoing need for more literature, programs, and resources addressing the underlying concerns.

Conclusion

In the beginning of the chapter, we met Seth, a pastor who left ministry following many challenges. The problem for Seth was not only his mental health struggles nor the challenges of ministry. The problem was also that he was alone in his struggles with no one addressing his needs. His story exemplifies both the importance of clergy care in general, as well as the significance of accurately identifying clergy needs and providing care that successfully addresses them. The needs of a clergyperson cannot be viewed holistically without understanding the roles, responsibilities, and commitments that are part of daily life and ministry. Therefore, programs and services intended to care for clergy need to consider the multiple demands and expectations that affect clergy every day, as well as the importance of relationships within their work context.

Ultimately, caring for clergy requires a systemic approach. We notice a pattern in the network of care providers. A lack of prioritization of clergy care may have a direct impact on the types and forms of programs and services that are provided. This pattern may have even more severe consequences for bivocational clergy, women clergy, and clergy of color. We have offered analysis of each sector and the needs that each sector addresses so that the providers can see the current disconnect within their network of providers. Our analysis shows how each sector specializes in meeting a few key areas of need yet fails to address others. We believe it is unrealistic that one sector or one care provider should meet every need for clergy. However, through awareness and collaboration, providers may understand their individual role, their complementary function, and their and other's support gaps.

Before beginning this collaboration, we recommend that each clergy care provider conduct a self-assessment of their programs and services. Fewer than half (43 percent) of our participants had surveyed their clergy for feedback in the past year.[17] This lack of feedback means that providers are missing out on valuable information pertaining to how effective they are in meeting the needs of those they serve. A self-assessment may help providers learn that some of their programs are ineffective. They can also assess potential new services, or areas they can refer to other providers.

After assessing their own strengths, clergy care providers will be in a better place to partner with others within their own sector and across other sectors. Partnership and collaboration can also enable clergy care providers to more effectively meet the needs of women clergy, bivocational clergy, and clergy of color. For example, our participants who work with bivocational clergy hope that there can be a normalization of the experience of bivocational clergy in predominantly white congregations; bivocationality has long been the norm for many communities of color. There is an opportunity there for clergy care providers within white communities to learn from providers within communities of color on how to best support bivocational clergy. Collaboration like this can be a difficult process, but when done correctly and with the right organizations, the outcome is more effective care and healthier clergy.

In the book of Exodus, Moses needed Aaron *and* Hur as the task at hand got wearisome and almost too hard to bear. Together, their support more holistically met the needs of Moses in a sustainable way. Likewise, Seth, and other clergy, may receive the support they need to navigate the challenges and loneliness of ministry if clergy care providers collaborate and work together.

17. Continuing education providers are much more likely to gather feedback since that is built into their practice as an institution. Counseling practices are the least likely to gather feedback.

7

Following the Money

IN THE EARLY 2000S, Helen, a Catholic sister who lived with other Catholic sisters at a retreat and conference center, learned that a private funder was providing grants to invest in the well-being of ordained clergy. Helen has a passion for supporting women. Because the grant specified "ordained" women and the Roman Catholic Church does not ordain women, Helen decided she would pursue grant funding to provide retreats for Protestant women clergy. She succeeded and secured money to design a program that created cohorts of women clergy from many theological traditions from across the United States. As a cohort, the women support each other and meet in person for three retreats for a year and a half. For nearly two decades, Helen has continued receiving grant money that supports women clergy across the United States.

Helen's story indicates the practical implications grants can have on the field of clergy care when providers have access to them. However, many of the largest granting organizations we have identified have geographic restrictions (or areas of concentration) where they invest their financial resources. Therefore, not everyone lives in locations where grant money is as easily accessible, nor, in many cases, do providers have the time it takes to write and apply for grant money. Consider Nick and Eloise, who recently started hosting retreats for clergy in the scenic Pacific Northwest. Providing retreats in these spaces is expensive. After we talked to them, they said that they wanted to expand their retreat center, but they do not know where to look for money or whether enough funding exists to support a larger endeavor. Many more clergy could benefit if Nick and Eloise had enough resources to grow their current operations or branch out in other locations.

Helen's and Nick and Eloise's stories resemble those of many in the field of clergy care across all sectors. Some providers have steady, relatively easy access to resources through grants, endowments, fees for service, or other sources such as denominations, while others, like Nick and Eloise, are constrained in what they can offer due to a lack of access to grant funding or money in general. As access to money can profoundly shape the type of programs offered and the care that clergy receive, we will examine the distribution of financial resources for clergy care providers by geography and sector.

The Role of Grants

Because of the power and influence that grants have on the field of clergy care, we investigated the grants issued by private foundations for clergy using data from IRS Form 990 from 2003 to 2019.[1] Conservatively, we estimate that 323 grantors issued 3,083 grants for clergy care totaling nearly $290 million over this period. These granting organizations range from large private foundations to family trusts, donor advised funds, and community foundations. Individual grants range from $25 to $12.2 million, with most grants (92 percent) less than $50,000 and 36 percent less than $10,000. The median grant issued between 2003 and 2019 totaled $38,000; however, since 2013 the median grant has been less than $10,000.

The following figure 7–1 illustrates the number of grants issued (illustrated by the line) and the amount of grant funding issued (illustrated by the columns).[2]

1. We coded any publicly available 990 from a foundation or granting organization that included the term clergy, minister, or pastor. However, it is possible that there are other broader terms like "ministry" that would yield different results. Therefore, we believe that our analysis produces the most conservative estimate and establishes a baseline but not a maximum for funding in the field. Further, many denominational foundations and agencies do not file 990s as religious institutions. Therefore, we are not able to account for these outside of our survey results.

2. The following analysis excludes two outsized grantors in the field. Although these organizations provide more than 80 percent of the funding available for clergy care, we have excluded them from our analysis in order to highlight the stories of other grantors and not just two organizations.

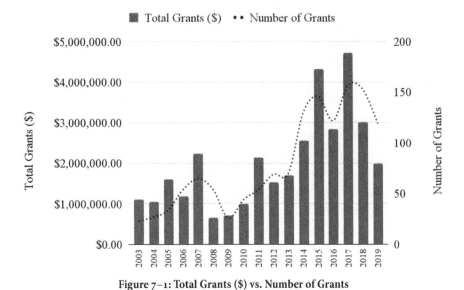

Figure 7–1: Total Grants ($) vs. Number of Grants

Until the 2008 Great Recession, the number of grants issued for clergy care steadily increased, while the amount of money granted remained relatively stable (though also potentially starting to increase prior to the Great Recession). The financial crisis of 2008 precipitously decreased both the total number of grants issued and the total dollar amount provided. Following the Great Recession, the amount of grant money available for clergy care fluctuated greatly. Fewer organizations received more money. As the economy improved between 2011 and 2013, philanthropic organizations increased their efforts both in terms of the number of grants issued and the total amount given.

Philanthropic foundations issue grants that care for clergy for a variety of purposes. Grantors provide funding for the benefit of clergy such as retreats, health and wellness resources, relief for financial distress, and housing assistance. Other funding is given for services such as education, discretionary funds, scholarships, conferences, and church resources. We categorized each of the grants into four general categories: economic, education, professional, and community benefit. Examples of each category include: (economic) money for the clergyperson to use for various purposes; (educational) conferences, scholarships; (professional) technology, staff support; and (community benefit) benevolence funds, advocacy.[3]

3. The categories are not mutually exclusive. A grant could be included in multiple categories.

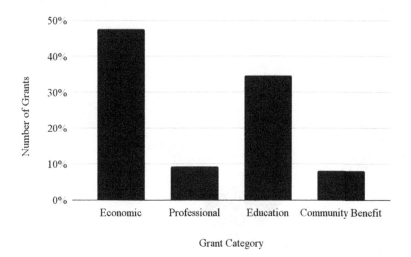

Figure 7-2: Distribution of Funding across Categories

As figure 7-2 shows, funding is not equally distributed across the subcategories. Economic and education categories dominate the grantors' interests. Often, economic grants are not restricted to specific purposes but can be used at the clergyperson's discretion. Educational grants primarily help the clergyperson or their staff advance their education. Professional purposes include, for example, new technology for the church or similar supplies. The community benefit category includes a range of uses such as refugee family assistance, benevolence funds, and ministries of the church in the community. Grantors provide funding to address a variety of purposes, but their main focus is on helping clergy with their economic and educational concerns.

Geographical Distribution of Resources

To determine how geography shapes the distribution of resources, we looked at the geographical distribution of resources to care for clergy by examining where grant funds are allocated to care for clergy.[4] Figure 7-3 shows the distribution across the United States of total grant funding. Given their relative population size, we see larger concentrations in Texas, New York, California, and parts of the Midwest. However, even though the

4. The following data comes from 2003-2019 990s filed with the IRS.

money is received in a particular location, it may be used to help clergy across North America.

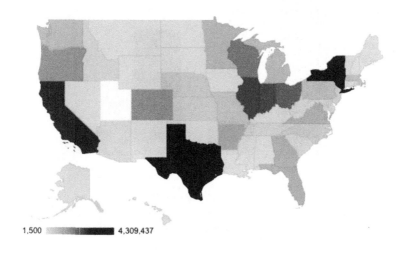

1,500 ▬▬▬▬ 4,309,437

Figure 7–3: Grant Distribution by State

We asked our survey participants to share the geographical areas where they provide services to further understand the distribution of resources. We asked about the scope of their organization's reach (international, national, regional, and local). Nearly 70 percent of organizations represented in our sample care for clergy either nationally or internationally (figure 7–4). Very few operate locally. Though many organizations operate with a small budget, technology enables them to reach clergy across North America. This may mean that although grant distributions vary by state, the resources are further distributed across North America, increasing access and availability to clergy in a way that is not constrained by geographical location.

We became aware of a story that highlights the significance of regional variation in the care that clergy receive. A benefit plan for a major American denomination offered a program for clergy, allowing them to receive counseling services and submit receipts through an insurance portal. Although this was a major benefit to many clergy within the denomination, there were only a handful of providers who accepted this form of insurance in entire regions of the country. Therefore, although the denominational office was providing a needed service, some clergy were practically unable to take advantage of this benefit. Awareness of how geography shapes access and availability of resources can show the additional steps clergy caregivers can take to improve the care for clergy.

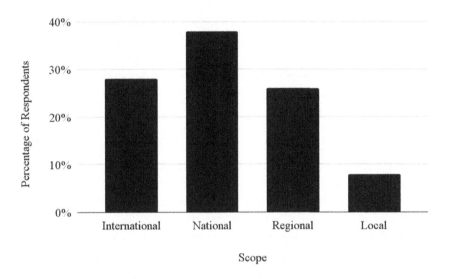

Figure 7–4: Geographic Scope of Programs and Services

Operating and Programmatic Budgets

Our survey revealed that a wide variety of organizations serve clergy, from large organizations to small organizations. Combined, the total annual operating budgets for all organizations represented in our sample exceed $6 billion. However, these financial resources are concentrated in a handful of organizations, with six organizations (mostly pension/benefit providers) accounting for 71 percent of total budgeted resources. As a result, these larger organizations inflate the field's average. While the average operating budget for organizations caring for clergy is $21.5 million, most organizations have much smaller budgets. Half of organizations have an operating budget of less than $775,000.[5] Ten percent of organizations (mostly retreat centers and people who volunteer to provide care for clergy in their local

5. More than 90 percent of our participants had a total organizational budget of less than $50 million.

churches) have an operating budget of less than $5,000, and 3 percent have no budget at all.

An organization's operating budget is also affected by the source(s) of funding upon which they draw. Having an endowment correlates with a larger operating budget than relying on donors alone. Clergy care providers funded by endowments include denominational foundations, seminaries, and some parachurch ministries. A reliable source of funding such as an endowment may increase a provider's confidence in exploring new innovative models. Clergy care providers who rely on donations and smaller operating budgets must spend more time seeking funding to sustain their operations and less on developing new programs and services for clergy.

Many organizations that fall within the broad network of clergy care serve a variety of clientele. As a result, differences often emerge between their total operating budget and the specific programmatic budget that they use for the care of clergy. Out of their operating budgets, organizations allocate "programmatic" funding. Programmatic funding refers to the funding associated with the programs or services that providers offer for clergy. For those organizations caring for clergy exclusively, programmatic budgets may be equivalent to 100 percent of the organization's operating budget. For example, Heartsprings Haven employs pastors to care for other pastors. Heartsprings Haven allocates nearly all of its budget for clergy care. For organizations that care for many types of clients (for example, counseling practices and many retreat centers), programmatic budgets may be only a small percentage of their operating budget. Figure 7–5 shows the breakdown of programmatic budgets by sector.

Despite the diversity of the field, programmatic budgets follow a similar trendline of crests and troughs across sectors. Almost 40 percent of organizations in our sample allocate between $100,000 and $500,000 of their operating budget on clergy care. Frontline providers and denominations, networks, and associations are more likely than other sectors to report that they have no programmatic budget to care for clergy.

In one way, this finding is understandable since frontline providers, like small counseling practices or retreat centers, may not allocate budgeted funds specifically to care for clergy. However, we are concerned that 15 percent of denominations, networks, and associations indicate no budget to care for their clergy. During our analysis, we anticipated denominational funding would be more influential in shaping the clergy served. Many denominations concentrate their support for clergy in either their pensions, benefit, and insurance organizations or in their denominational foundations. Outside of these sectors, our research reveals that many denominations provide minimal funding for clergy support. Considering that historically the institution of the church once had sole responsibility for caring for clergy, it is remarkable that a sizable minority of denominations, networks, and associations do not allocate money for the care of clergy.

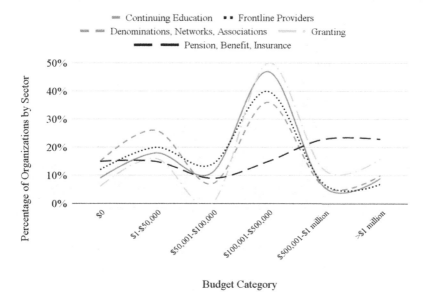

Figure 7–5: Budget for Clergy by Sector

The pension, benefit, and insurance sector is unique. This sector does not follow the standard pattern across programmatic asset classes. It is the only sector where the number of organizations in each category increases slightly throughout the programmatic budget ranges. Whereas all other sectors have the largest proportion of their organizations represented in the $100,001–$500,000 category, nearly half of the pension, benefit, and insurance providers have a clergy care budget of more than $500,000. Organizations from other sectors serve a variety of clientele and allocate their budgeted resources accordingly.

Addressing the various needs of clergy may add additional strain to already tight budgets. Most organizations allocate only a fraction of their operating budget to care for clergy. We estimate that more than half of organizations (56 percent) in our sample devote less than 25 percent of their operating budgets to caring for clergy (figure 7–6). Only 12 percent of these organizations allocate between 76 to 100 percent of their operational budget to the care of clergy.[6] We also find variation by asset class. No organization with an operating budget of more than $500,000 allocates their total operating budget to the care of clergy. In fact, no organization in this higher asset class allocates more than 60 percent of its budget to the care of clergy.

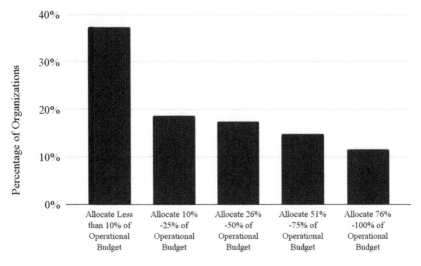

Figure 7–6: Estimated Programmatic Budgets

Funding Sources

Most organizations have an average of two sources of funding. For example, many continuing education institutions receive funding from both grants and fees for service (e.g., tuition). Although nearly half of organizations receive funding from grants, only 15 percent of organizations receive funding from congregations. Congregations might care for clergy in more informal, local, and personal ways. However, the typical congregation may not have

6. Participants who indicated that their programmatic budget exceeded their operational budget are excluded from this analysis. Our data do not permit a direct comparison between operational and programmatic budgets because our survey asked our participants to provide a numerical value for their operating budget but select a budget category for their programmatic budget (see appendix B). The 12 percent includes volunteers who do not have a budget, some retreat centers, and other organizations created specifically to care for clergy.

the funds required to sponsor a clergy care program, or if they do, they may not believe that they have responsibility to sponsor programs for clergy beyond their local congregation.

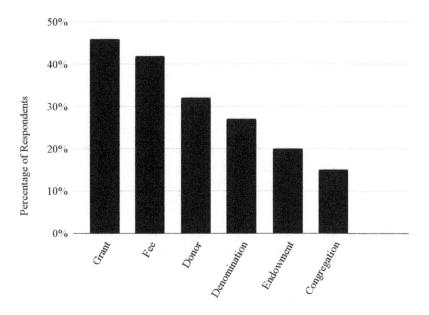

Figure 7–7: Source of Funding

Although no single funding source dominates the field of clergy care across sectors, the source of an organization's funding plays a role in shaping the activity, programs, and services that clergy receive, as well as who is served. Clergy care organizations that receive funding from grants are twice as likely to serve bivocational clergy when compared to those who do not receive funding from grants.[7] Resource centers and continuing education providers are twice as likely as other sectors to receive funding from grants. As a result, these sectors are three times more likely to serve bivocational clergy when compared to other sectors.[8] Consistent with our findings above, denominational sources are a smaller source of funding for clergy care than other sources like grants or fees for service.

7. These results are similar for part-time clergy.

8. Pension, benefit, and insurance providers are half as likely to receive funding from grants and are slightly less likely to offer programs and services that cater to the needs of bivocational clergy. Pension, benefit, and insurance organizations are twice as likely to rely on endowments.

The source of an organization's funding impacts the needs providers address. In chapter 6, we discussed how an organization's sector affects the needs that clergy caregivers address. Clergy care providers are nearly twice as likely to address financial needs (e.g., underwriting care costs, educational scholarships, medical bills, debt, or financial training) if they receive funding from grants, compared to those who do not receive funding from grants. However, if the provider receives funding from congregations, they are nearly four times as likely to address financial needs compared to those who do not receive funding from congregations. We hypothesize that the more local a funding source the greater impact it has on the specific need that providers address. This finding may have significance for the way that philanthropy is executed. When financial support is rooted locally, then it may be more likely clergy care providers treat the root cause of clergy health rather than the symptom, having a greater and more lasting impact (see ch. 5).

Is the Budget Enough?

In addition to our interest in the amount of funding available for clergy care, we also sought to determine if our participants believed that the amount of funding was enough to sufficiently care for clergy. Approximately 55 percent of our participants believe their budget is not sufficient for the care that needs to be provided. The proportion of those who do not believe they have enough budget varies by sector and types of care provided. We identified two key factors that affect whether a participant believes the budget is enough: the funding source and previous pastoral experience.

Some sources of funding may be more sufficient and reliable than others. When the source of funding is reliable, participants are more likely to believe that they have enough funding. Participants funded by endowments are statistically more than three times as likely to say the budget is enough to care for clergy compared to those who are not funded by endowments. Participants funded by donors and/or denominations are the least likely to say the budget for clergy is enough. When compared to an endowment, funding from donors and denominations may be more variable and provide fewer dollars for clergy care. The dependability of different sources of funding varies by sector and may prompt perceptions of scarcity, sufficiency, or abundance.

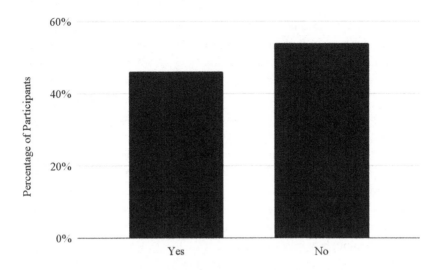

Figure 7–8: Is the Budget Enough?

Previous pastoral experience also affects how participants perceive the sufficiency of the money they have to provide care for clergy. More than 60 percent of those with previous pastoral experience think that their budget to care for clergy is not enough.[9] Previous pastors may overestimate the amount of money needed for clergy care, although we hypothesize that those with previous pastoral experience have personal knowledge of the needs of clergy, which may give them a more intimate understanding of the needs that clergy have. Conversely, not having previous pastoral experience may limit the understanding of the provider in seeing the full range of needs that clergy have or in accurately estimating the amount of money needed to adequately care for clergy. This might explain why some professions (counseling practices, retreat center hosts, etc.) are more likely to say that the budget is not enough. These professions both attract more previous pastors as employees and are more likely than other sectors to say that the budget is not enough.

9. Previous pastoral experience has a statistically significant relationship with believing that the budget is not enough. Also, fewer than 40 percent of those who do not have previous pastoral experience think that their budget is not enough.

Conclusion

This chapter assesses the profound role of funders and granting organizations in shaping which clergy receive care and how their care is provided. Helen could not have impacted as many clergy women as she had without the ongoing support from her grants. Overall, our results suggest that some providers are confident their programs and services are adequately funded to care for clergy. However, this confidence is largely due to reliable sources of funding and the lack of personal familiarity with the needs of clergy. Thus, confidence is not evenly distributed across the field of clergy care. Nick, particularly, lacked confidence that he could find enough funding. However, the disproportionate distribution of money is not always a bad thing. Sometimes certain providers have more expenses, serve more clergy, and need more money than others. However, in some cases it can result in providers not having enough money to effectively care for the clergy they serve.

We hope that our analysis of how resources are distributed to care for clergy will be a catalyst for further investigation. We call for research into both the sufficiency of budgets intended for clergy care as well as the efficacy of programs and services meeting clergy needs. As the church in North America changes, we anticipate that financial resources will be an increasing concern not only for clergy but also for institutions and organizations who care for clergy. Once-stable denominational bodies have been dramatically impacted by changes in religious affiliation, financial giving, and, in some cases, schism. As a result, clergy may be left without the same safety net that they would have had just a generation ago. With shifts, like the one we noted in chapter 6 toward bivocational ministry, the field of clergy care needs to strategically plan for shifts in resource allocation and develop sustainable models for the future.

8

What's Getting in the Way?

IN A SEASON OF discernment, God placed a dream within Erica's heart to start a center providing spiritual direction and wraparound care for clergy. She made this dream the focus of her doctor of ministry thesis and had aspirations to become a frontline provider. With excitement, she prepared a glossy brochure and a detailed business plan for the head of her regional denominational body. After sharing her dream with this denominational official, he said, "Erica, this is a great idea, but I just don't have time to support it." Undeterred, Erica tried to think creatively of others who could endorse and support her ministry. She published her dissertation as a book and sent it to a number of influential denominational officials along with a request for comment. She never got a response from any of them.

Erica persisted. She applied for and received nonprofit status for her organization and began building grassroots support. However, because she had a preexisting condition, Erica needed health insurance. She knew that her denomination had a special status that would allow her to maintain her denominational health insurance while pursuing her dream of providing care for clergy. However, the board overseeing that status denied her petition. It seemed like everyone could say no, but no one was willing to say yes. Erica persevered and eventually established her organization, but the journey to get there was full of frustrating setbacks and roadblocks.

These roadblocks can come from professional sources, like the ones Erica experienced, or they can be more connected to structural sources that are part of cultural realities. For example, something as simple as location can make offering in-person programming difficult, especially for providers serving minority clergy. Consider Michelle, a Black clergy care provider who works with evangelical clergy women. As part of her ministry, Michelle hosts annual in-person retreats but struggles to find a location where the women feel safe. She used to host her gatherings at a retreat center in a rural setting. The retreat center itself was welcoming. However, when the women traveled to nearby towns during their free time, they shared that they often experienced implicit or explicit racism. Michelle noted that in these settings the anxiety for participants increased—the opposite of what her retreat intended to accomplish. Michelle struggles to find a retreat center that is not only welcoming to clergy women of color but is also located in an area that welcomes them too.

We frequently heard stories like those of Erica and Michelle. At least 20 percent of clergy care providers currently encounter roadblocks in their ministry. As a result, one in five clergy care providers may be feeling discouraged in their work at any given time. Many have experienced roadblocks in the past or will experience them in the future. Further, we have evidence to suggest that this number is higher among underserved populations where budgets are smaller.[1] Many providers, like Erica and Michelle, need encouragement, which may be found through partnership and collaboration. In this chapter, we explore two key roadblocks: professional and structural.

Professional Roadblocks

Providers encounter professional roadblocks related to time, money, and people. Lack of funding or lack of time comprise nearly 50 percent of the professional roadblocks clergy care providers experience. As we described in chapter 7, this is due to the reality that many organizations devote only a fraction of their budget to caring for clergy. The clergy care providers within these organizations must advocate for time and money to serve

1. We conducted a focus group to further explore these roadblocks, and a number of their responses addressed organizations that do not prioritize clergy care. For the focus group, we randomly selected participants from those who indicated that they encountered roadblocks in their work. We asked questions concerning how they would describe the roadblocks, how they personally were affected by roadblocks, and what has or has not worked when addressing roadblocks.

clergy. Forty-seven percent of our participants serve clergy part-time.[2] Of those who care for clergy part-time, 40 percent spend less than five hours a week serving clergy. Many of these providers do not have the time to care for clergy as much as they desire because of lack of priority and vision, competing priorities, and multiple responsibilities.

Some of our participants believe that the lack of time and funding is a smokescreen. In other words, organizations might say they care about clergy and also say they do not have enough time and money to prioritize programs or services for clergy. In reality, the organizations may be able to do more to invest time and money for clergy, but they concentrate on other priorities. Our participants suggested that funders could play a major role in working alongside organizations to better prioritize the support of clergy. As we saw in the last chapter, funders invest significant resources in clergy care. If funders strategically invest their resources, they could help alleviate some of the major roadblocks providers of clergy care often encounter.

Besides time and money, the other 50 percent of professional road-blocks relate to individuals (such as clergy and laity) and dynamics associated with the congregations they serve. Lacking self-awareness, clergy often deny that they need care, and providers sometimes struggle to persuade them to receive the care they offer. Consider Robert, who runs a resource center that has curated programs for clergy. Robert does not understand why clergy do not seem interested in using his services. Although many clergy affirm Robert's work, these same clergy believe that they do not personally need Robert's services. Even when clergy are aware of their needs, they may not have the necessary resources of time and money to seek care. Now, Robert is planning to decrease the time he spends each week with the resource center and move into other areas of ministry.

Lisa oversees her denomination's ordination requirements. She has the responsibility of assessing candidates' readiness for ministry and their calling to become pastors. In her experience, some candidates need therapy and counseling before she feels comfortable recommending them for ordination. Lisa shared a story with us about a candidate who struggled with depression as a result of grief due to a loss she experienced. Lisa recommended counseling for the candidate to address this previous hurt and the trauma associated with it. Although the candidate met with the counselor, the candidate discussed frustrations with her ministry and avoided topics

2. One in three work more than ten hours a week to care for clergy.

associated with her grief. In this instance, the candidate either was not ready to address her grief or resisted help in doing so.

Laity may have unrealistic expectations of clergy, requiring clergy to be on call 24/7 with little time for the clergyperson's own self-care.[3] Howard leads a clergy care organization helping congregations address conflict. His ministry involves coaching clergy and providing them with practical tools to address challenges in their congregations through extended off-site training and workshops. Howard has experienced some laity who believe that these extra programs would "distract" their pastor from other more important responsibilities. According to some of the laity with whom Howard has spoken, they do not want their pastor to spend time away from his or her primary duties associated with their congregation. As above, lay leaders may also be resistant to allocating funds from the congregation's already tight budget for professional development.

Structural Roadblocks

Structural roadblocks are rooted in systemic inequalities, often associated with economic and cultural disparities. Clergy care providers encounter structural roadblocks in their work associated with women clergy, clergy of color, and bivocational clergy. The "stained-glass ceiling" refers to the structural roadblock for women to be seen as effective leaders in the church and thus unable to obtain more significant positions (such as a lead pastor position in larger congregations). The stained-glass ceiling can also affect the financial resources of women clergy. Research has found that women clergy earn $0.93 to every dollar that men earn. Although the compensation ratio has improved over the past few decades, a significant proportion of that improvement was due to slowing gains for men's income.[4]

Even when congregations have no formal measures in place to exclude women in leadership, congregations may still hold on to what scholars refer to as symbolic cultural norms.[5] Congregations may signal that

3. See also Proeschold-Bell and Byassee, *Faithful and Fractured*, 4.

4. Adams, "Stained Glass."

5. It is assumed that a male leader is more impersonal, rational, and task-oriented while women tend to be more nurturing, flexible, and communal in their leadership styles (Lehman, *Gender and Ministry Style*). Sociologist and Episcopal priest Gail Cafferata observes, "Like women in other occupations, women pastors may be more inclined to exercise charismatic or inspirational personal authority and to see themselves as empathic, transformational leaders. . . . In contrast, prevailing gender norms make it

they follow more traditional gender roles by filling top positions within the church with men. While culture does affect congregants' expectations of women clergy, research has shown that ideology and theology play roles in these expectations.[6] Women clergy and those who provide services and programs for them have to confront and overcome these roadblocks to effectively perform their role as ministers. Yet, as with the limited scope of literature we identified for or about women clergy in chapter 4, there are relatively few programs for women in ministry. As one of our participants noted, "Mentorship matters for women in ministry. For a lot of women coming out of seminary, there is nothing out there for you, especially in church positions." In chapter 6, we observed how few providers address relational needs, exacerbating the struggles of loneliness and isolation often experienced by underrepresented populations, especially women and clergy of color.[7]

Women are not the only clergy population affected by structural roadblocks. Andy is a continuing education provider who began seeing the need for more research on bivocational clergy after learning from the experiences of bivocational students in his classroom. He noted that some denominations have written in their by-laws that bivocationality is outside of the norm of what constitutes proper ministry. These theological traditions see bivocational ministry as an outcome of declining denominational membership and congregations who cannot afford a full-time pastor. Andy sees these institutional provisions as creating structural bias that delegitimizes those with a bivocational career.

For other traditions especially within minority communities, bivocational ministry has long been the norm. A 2017 survey conducted by ATS found that 30 percent of seminary graduates planned on serving in

---

easier for male clergy to exercise a transactional or laissez-faire leadership style where relationships are more formal, exchange-based, and focused on task completion. One study found that nearly a third of women pastors view their role primarily as one of empowering laity to implement decisions that laity have made, whereas only 10 percent of clergy men chose this style (Carroll 2006) . . . women leaders are seen as more effective when they exercise both inspirational motivation (seen as agentic) and individual consideration (that is seen as communal)." Cafferata, "Gender, Judicatory Respect." Also see Proeschold-Bell and Byassee, *Faithful and Fractured*, 146–47.

6. Cafferata, "Gender, Judicatory Respect."

7. Proeschold-Bell and Byassee find that when African American clergy experience poor mental health, they first seek support from other African American clergy, even though that support can be hard to find in more rural or remote areas. Proeschold-Bell and Byassee, *Faithful and Fractured*, 152.

bivocational ministry.[8] However, the percentage of graduates considering bivocational ministry increased among minority communities. Fifty-seven percent of Black graduates planned on serving in bivocational ministry.[9] Half of Black seminary graduates have a debt of over $20,000, and only a third of Black seminary graduates expect to be "fairly and adequately compensated as a professional."[10] As bivocationality becomes more the norm for ministry, we expect that the issue of addressing seminary debt will continue to be an issue for those providing care for clergy.

Raul, who is a denominational official, works with Hispanic bivocational clergy in the Central United States. Raul grew up in a first-generation Hispanic congregation and later served as a bivocational minister while he pursued an advanced degree. In his current role, Raul assists bivocational Hispanic clergy with their legal difficulties, finances, and other hardships in the ministry. Raul supports bivocational clergy who yearn for more education. However, he has found that many clergy resources are not available in Spanish.

Raul must single-handedly translate resources for the clergy he serves so that they can have access to these resources. Additionally, Raul pointed out that the programs and services designed for full-time clergy are not often as accessible to bivocational clergy. For instance, many bivocational clergy cannot just leave for a workweek or even a weekend to attend a clergy retreat. Raul finds that much of his time in caring for bivocational clergy is helping them to navigate the structural roadblocks they face in being effective in their ministry. And consequently, those roadblocks, such as the lack of materials in Spanish, affect Raul's ability to provide effective care for clergy.

When clergy serve in a bivocational capacity, sabbaticals are usually off the table. It is hard to take time off from either their church or secular jobs. In addition to these factors associated with secular employment and the demands of ministry, the financial cost to attend a retreat or similar type of gathering is often too great a burden. For the clergy Raul serves, making $10,000–$16,000 a year is respectable. In some cases, the clergy he serves do not receive a salary. Raul pours endless hours into helping his clergy be effective ministers and take care of themselves and their families

8. Deasy, "Graduating Student Questionnaire."

9. Further, 41 percent of Latinx and 34 percent of First Nation graduates planned to serve in bivocational ministry.

10. Banks, "Black Seminary Grads."

at the same time. He longs to see bivocational clergy access more resources and support.

Like Raul, Naomi also noticed that bivocational clergy have trouble finding time to fully access available resources. Naomi is a researcher and psychologist who offers counseling services for clergy. She conducted a study of Black bivocational ministers. However, she found it difficult to arrange the interviews because these clergy often did not have time. Between their ministry for the church, outside employment, and family responsibilities, she found that bivocational ministers have little free time. To make matters worse, many congregations expect their pastor, even if they are bivocational or part-time, to be on call for the congregation 24/7.

Bivocational clergy navigate complex responsibilities and time commitments and do so while caring for their family and prioritizing their relationship with God. However, providers assert the importance of maintaining healthy boundaries in bivocational ministry. As a result of the growth in bivocational ministry, continuing education providers have begun offering more classes on evenings and weekends. Asynchronous classes can also make education more available to clergy who work long hours and need greater flexibility to complete a degree in their own timing. Educating bivocational clergy requires flexibility on the part of those providing care. Not all clergy care providers can offer such flexibility, but from those who can, we heard them tell of the great reward in working with bivocational clergy.

Structural inequities mean that tragedies such as the COVID-19 pandemic add additional strain for marginalized communities on top of what everyone else suffers. The COVID-19 pandemic both exposed and exacerbated the structural inequities that shape access to availability of support for these populations. Michelle, the Black woman we introduced at the beginning of this chapter, also works with a seminary. She focuses her ministry on supporting women, especially women of color. Following the onset of the COVID-19 pandemic, she received numerous messages from women clergy with a noticeable shift from complaints to signals of distress. The women with whom she works often have fewer opportunities for leadership and preaching in the church. After the pandemic, the women still had those complaints with the addition of extreme exhaustion and declining health. In addition to the extra time and fewer resources, clergy care providers like Raul, Naomi, and Andy often feel isolated and alone because the concerns they deal with are not the same as those who provide services for majority populations. Effectively addressing structural barriers requires a systemic approach, with clergy care providers working together, collaborating, and partnering to support underserved populations.

Some Strategies for Overcoming Roadblocks

While professional and structural roadblocks discourage many of our participants, there is hope. Our participants shared strategies they incorporate into their work that help them overcome roadblocks.[11] Many of these strategies come from lived experiences of convincing individuals and organizations why clergy care matters. The two most common strategies for overcoming roadblocks include having the right data and endorsements. First, providers need reliable sources of empirical data to help orient and benchmark their ministry. Our research about clergy well-being underscores the importance of academic scholarship in both understanding trends but also in establishing an evidence base to support the care providers offer. Second, clergy care providers rely on endorsements from influential individuals and institutions. When a well-known pastor, denominational official, or other notable figure has endorsed a provider's service, clergy may be more willing to participate.

Some participants find that having a clergyperson model the actions of both seeking and receiving care is important. Clergy are more likely to engage if a provider can point to someone who has benefited from one of their programs, especially within a peer group. Sharing testimonials of the experiences of these individuals or the provider's personal experience receiving care helps highlight the benefit of such care. Since 70 percent of our participants include former pastors, providers may have personal stories from their own ministry about how receiving care helped or about how not receiving care led to detrimental effects. In both survey data and interviews, providers noted the importance of naming the benefits of a program or service not only to the individual clergyperson but also to their ministry. Clergy want to know that the care they receive increases their effectiveness in ministry. As pastoral counselor and coach Denny Howard writes, "We serve no one well when we live frantic, overloaded, and exhausted lives."[12] Our participants assert that clergy can better minister to others when the clergy receive the support and care they need. These strategies require

11. We asked all of our participants to provide the strategies they incorporate to address roadblocks, regardless of whether they experience them or not.

12. Howard, *At Full Strength*, 309.

effective communication that is grounded in personal experience and backed up by data, when possible.

Even though finances are a major source of professional roadblocks, fewer than 10 percent of participants said that financial incentives were a strategy to overcome both professional and structural roadblocks. Yet, clergy need financial resources and/or tangible benefits. For example, a financial scholarship to help bivocational clergy take time off from both of their careers may be required for participation. Tangible benefits such as childcare may also increase participation.

As noted by less than 2 percent of the total responses, our participants barely relied on Scripture or theology as a strategy of overcoming roadblocks. We expected to see a greater emphasis on biblical or theological rationales. The network of clergy care providers has the opportunity to develop a robust theology of clergy care, rooted in God's love for clergy and the calling of the body of Christ to care for its leaders.

Conclusion

Through our research, we have identified contributing factors associated with roadblocks. Providers who have a stable source of funding do not encounter as many professional barriers as those who must continually raise funds. Some organizational types are more likely to experience roadblocks than others. For instance, participants from resource centers are twice as likely to experience roadblocks when compared to participants from other types of organizations. Additionally, the source of an organization's funding affects whether participants experience roadblocks. Clergy care providers funded by denominations are three times more likely to experience roadblocks than other clergy care providers. Finally, organizations funded by endowments were the least likely to experience roadblocks. Organizations will always try to find resources to invest in their priorities. If they prioritize the well-being of clergy, they will allocate resources to invest in clergy well-being.

Although the strategies our participants identified may help address the roadblocks clergy care providers encounter, a systemic approach is needed to effectively mobilize resources, dedicate time, and funnel energy to make the care of clergy a priority. The process of assuring that clergy and their providers have sufficient funding requires strategic allocation of resources, with particular attention to bivocational clergy, women clergy, and clergy of color. However, there will never be enough time, money, or people for "causes" that are not viewed as a priority. Taking a systemic approach not only requires attention to the professional and structural roadblocks encountered by providers, but also the institutional cultures, priorities, and values that produce these roadblocks.

In the beginning of this chapter, we met Erica who wrestled for years with her denomination to establish an organization that cares for clergy. Erica now leads that organization, but the road to get there was filled with repeated roadblocks. She persisted because she believed that God gave her a vision. Yet, in the pursuit of her dream, Erica could have used practical strategies to navigate the complex dynamics associated with her denomination. Additionally, she could have used some friends.

We have identified a number of clergy care providers who feel alone and discouraged in their work. Clergy care providers can overcome roadblocks and persevere through setbacks if they have a community upon which they can rely. They need support themselves. If they band together, providers can share ideas, solve problems, come up with innovative solutions, and carry each other's burdens.

9

Conclusion

WHAT WOULD HAVE HAPPENED in the book of Exodus if Aaron and Hur had been unable to provide adequate support for Moses when he grew tired? What if these supporters had had no imagination for the significance of what Moses was doing or what their roles supporting him could accomplish? Furthermore, what if they had been uncoordinated like the NGOs in Haiti, each with a separate agenda, without a shared language, or a common understanding of what needed to be done and how to do it? The implications of a lack of vision for their role, as well as a lack of coordination, could have been tremendous. A defeat in this battle would have delayed Israel's entrance into the promised land and changed the subsequent history of the people of God.

Aaron and Hur played a critical role collectively upholding the arms of Moses and, by virtue of that, supporting the entire nation of Israel. Similarly, the support clergy care providers offer today is critical and benefits more than just clergy. Indirectly, their efforts benefit the congregations and communities clergy serve. In this book, we have identified five sectors that care for clergy at scale. As we stated in chapter 1, we conservatively estimate that the providers we sampled support more than half of the Protestant clergy in the United States. These clergy, in turn, provide leadership to congregations across the United States and Canada. The systemic impact these providers have collectively is staggering. Their investment of time, energy, and resources buttress the ministry of congregations and has the capability to produce an exponential return for the kingdom of God.

Simply put, the ministry of clergy care providers matters. Since the days of the Exodus, the Judeo-Christian heritage has affirmed this position. The people of God have provided direct assistance, established common expectations for support, and developed institutions to ensure that clergy have what they need. Throughout the centuries, there have been individuals moved by God to support those in ministry. This support has become more critical during the past few years as religious disaffiliation has increased and we have observed the impact of growing secularization, mental health concerns, partisan battles, and a global pandemic.

The coordination of this network of clergy care providers also matters. One of our participants described the network of clergy care providers as it currently stands like the "Wild West," filled with well-meaning lone rangers. More often than not, we find siloed conversations, few individuals reading the same things, no shared agreement of a common language, or an understanding of the root causes driving their work. If collaboration occurs, we find it often limited to specific denominational or theological traditions, granting networks, or particular sectors. Like the NGOs in Haiti, clergy care providers are disconnected, hindering the effectiveness of their collective ministry.

Instead of operating in individual silos, the network of clergy care providers has the opportunity to operate as the communal body of Christ. In 1 Cor 12, Paul describes different parts of the body and underscores their need for one another. One member—like the foot—cannot say to another member—such as the hand—that they do not belong and have no use. According to Paul, the church should function like the human body: diverse members working in harmony with specific tasks and different roles to play.

Likewise, each organization within each sector providing clergy care has a unique function and purpose. Their diversity and specialization highlight the range of needs that clergy have. This diversity adds benefit to the programs and services clergy receive. Together, they are stronger and more effective than they are apart.

We do not suggest that every organization needs to be an expert in or responsible for every type of support for clergy. However, we do suggest that, at minimum, clergy care providers be aware of other organizations (especially those in other sectors) and, at best, coordinate their efforts where possible. If they do, clergy care providers may learn from each other, engage in mutual support, share best practices, celebrate excellence, innovate, and establish minimum standards of care.

In order to fulfill this challenging and complex role, we recognize that clergy care providers need their own support, training, and community. Individually, we find that many clergy care providers lack formational experiences or training to perform the work they feel called to do. Some lack formal goals for their programs and services and have not surveyed the clergy they serve to understand their needs, nor do they understand how their conceptualization of clergy well-being affects the care they provide. Training could significantly help these providers be more effective and efficient in their work. Additionally, a number of clergy care providers still have open, untreated wounds themselves from previous experiences inside and outside the church. They are in need of support as well as healing.

Danger exists in ignoring these warning signs, not only for providers and the clergy they serve but also for the reputation and witness of the church. Professor of preaching J. Ellsworth Kalas once said, "Beware of serving the bread of life with emaciated hands." Some participants expressed loneliness, isolation, or personal discouragement. These providers need the companionship found within community to bolster their spirits and drive their continued passion to care for clergy.

Although we find the vast majority of participants interested in this kind of community, unfortunately, on occasion we have identified some organizations and individuals who do not see the benefit of it, even when goals and missions are aligned. At times, this reticence extends out of an aversion to working alongside those from different denominational or theological traditions or from a fear of competition. More often, we find the reasons to be more mundane: the tyranny of the urgent, a belief that "my way is the only way," and limited resources of either time or money. As a result, these factors hinder collaboration and prohibit providers from fully engaging with others. We must resist this pull and intentionally run towards one another, for we are at a critical juncture in the life of the church.

If we want our leaders to be healthy and supported, the existing network of clergy care providers needs to be strengthened, revitalized, and grown. To achieve this end will require postures of openness and shared values. Providers will need to invest in relationships with other providers, build trust, and establish cultures of humility, generosity, and collaboration. They will need to realize that they need others to achieve their goals and believe that their work is part of something bigger than themselves.

Ultimately, these individual and corporate decisions about how, when, and if clergy care providers collaborate, work on problems together, and share ideas will reveal something about what they value and believe. With whom can I work? From whom can I learn? Who is an appropriate partner? Do I believe in a mission larger than my individual efforts? The way that clergy care providers answer these questions is an expression of practical theology manifest in their priorities as well as their day-to-day actions. It speaks to their ethics, ecclesiology, and understanding of the mission of God.

If clergy care providers remain steadfast and make this commitment, then clergy will be better supported, the church has the potential to be more effective, and the reign of God will be more visible in our midst. If healthy leadership is a fundamental requirement for healthy congregations, what message does it send to the world if the church has unhealthy, unsupported leaders? How many people have left the faith because the pressures of ministry created a toxic environment that does not reflect the will of God? If we go down a path where the church reflects a dysfunctional institution manifested first and foremost within positions of leadership and authority, the credibility and witness of the church is tarnished. By contrast, consider what it would be like if society looked to the church to understand how to best care for its leaders. As theologian Miroslav Volf maintains:

> World religions stand or fall on their ability to connect people to the transcendent realm and thereby make it possible for them to truly flourish, to find genuine fulfillment in both their successes and failures, and to lead lives worthy of human beings, lives marked by joyous contentment and solidarity.[1]

The work performed by clergy care providers embodies the ministry of human flourishing, which is a fundamental requirement for the church's public witness.

If we choose to work toward these goals, we have the potential to change the tide of the battle and promote flourishing not only within our congregations but within the world. We have what we need. Clergy care providers have passion for their ministry. They care about clergy and the service they provide and are called to this work. They have the spirit of God to guide and direct them. They rely on the depth of their faith and a Christian tradition of caring for the whole person.

---

1. Volf, *Flourishing*, 81–82.

Conclusion

If we remain true to these values and work toward these goals, we envision fewer headlines about crises within the church and more headlines about how clergy and congregations are contributing to the thriving of their communities. We see new pipelines for young people considering vocational ministry, knowing that they will be cared for and supported. We envision a more connected network of clergy care providers offering more effective support for clergy in need.

We imagine virtuous cycles of research and practice leading to interventions and innovations in clergy care and a growing literature on clergy that providers can use to inform and guide their practices, especially literature for and by underserved populations such as women clergy, bivocational clergy, clergy of color, and non-English speakers. We see the importance of empirically based programs. Institutions will offer certificates and continuing education seminars to provide clergy care providers to improve the care they offer.

Now is the time to act. Whether you are a clergy care provider, a clergyperson, or a lay reader, we invite you to respond to the challenges and opportunities we have outlined in this book. One practical first step we want to offer is an invitation to explore the Common Table Collaborative. In the midst of the COVID-19 pandemic and alongside this research, the Ormond Center at Duke Divinity School along with partners at the Clergy Health Initiative, Azusa Pacific University, and the Wesleyan Church came together to establish the Common Table Collaborative, which stewards connections among friends in North America who are called to clergy and congregational well-being. The goal of the Common Table is to break down silos, increase collaboration, and build friendships among partners committed to caring for clergy and congregations. We invite you to check out the resources we have begun to curate both online and in-person. You can find out more at the Common Table website: https://commontable.network.

Appendix A

Methodology

THE CARING FOR CLERGY research is the first large-scale study of the individuals and institutions that care for clergy within the United States and parts of Canada. We have developed what we believe is the most comprehensive and up to date database of Protestant clergy care providers in North America. Additionally, we conducted a yearlong research study, drawing upon qualitative interviews, focus groups, site visits, and a quantitative survey. Since our research launched on June 11, 2021, 394 participants have completed a self-administered survey. Our survey garnered a 47 percent response rate, and, on average, our participants completed the survey in 25 minutes.[1] Underscoring the significance of this statistic, we did not offer compensation or incentives for completing the survey. We believe that this positive reception is due in part to our personalized outreach to participants. We personally contacted 740 participants and followed up with them one to two times. However, our participants were eager to engage the survey due to our partnerships with key networks and organizations (such as the Association of Theological Schools [ATS] and the Church Benefits Association); endorsements from leaders in the field of clergy caregiving; and, ultimately, the excitement, desire, and the need that our participants have noted for this research. After completing our survey, numerous participants sent our office e-mails thanking us for conducting this study,

1. Some who were ineligible to take the survey because they do not provide programs or services for clergy took only a few minutes, while others spent over an hour completing the survey.

asking to be notified when analysis is complete, and describing the critical need for this research they see in their own ministry.

The first part of the project began in June 2020 with focus groups composed of academic and professional leaders whose work focuses on clergy from a broad spectrum of institutional settings, theological traditions, geographic areas, and racial/ethnic backgrounds. We wanted to understand how researchers and providers understood clergy well-being. After our analysis, we tested and validated our results in a series of virtual focus groups hosted by the Common Table Collaborative in December 2020.

From January 2021 to January 2022, we regularly convened both academic and professional advisory boards composed of a diverse set of industry-leading practitioners and scholars of clergy care and clergy well-being. These groups assisted us in designing our aims, defining our research questions, testing and publicizing our survey, and helping us to understand the significance of our work from a theological, organizational, and societal perspective.

Our team first defined the terms that we were using. In order to understand the support network available to clergy, one must understand the term "clergy." This professional identification has a broad meaning across and within religious traditions. For instance, clergy perform ministerial functions in different settings such as hospitals, business corporations, nonprofit organizations, branches of the armed services, denominational bodies, and local congregations. Some clergy are students, while others are active or retired. We mapped some of the major ways that the term clergy could be understood and identified as our primary focus those persons who supported clergy, with clergy defined as minister in a congregational setting, whether ordained or not. We also included part-time and bivocational clergy so long as they ministered to a congregation at least part-time (see appendix A–1).

Since our study is the first of its kind, boundaries were needed to anchor our analysis. We decided to focus our research on the network supporting Protestant clergy. In addition to Protestant clergy ranking as the most numerous in the United States,[2] ample diversity exists across theological, organizational, political, and racial/ethnic lines. Protestantism offers enough similarity for comparative analysis while still maintaining a fair degree of complexity and variation. Additionally, we felt that our analysis would be sharper and more actionable if we focused on Protestants before

2. See United States Cenus Bureau, "American Community Survey"; National Congregations Study, "National Survey of Religious Leaders."

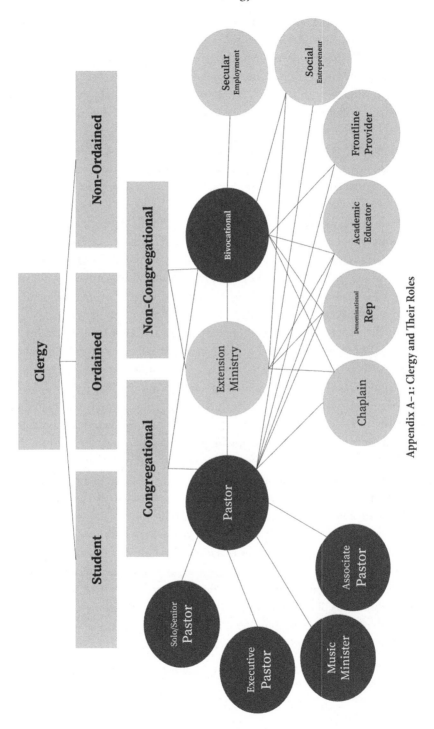

Appendix A–1: Clergy and Their Roles

trying to assess the network of clergy care providers in other religious traditions. We hope that future research will examine these networks in Roman Catholic, Orthodox, Jewish, Muslim, and other religious traditions.

Next, we defined the type of providers offering care for clergy. Clergy are surrounded by those who care about their well-being in small, unstructured, and often informal ways. For example, families cook meals or send notes of encouragement to their pastors. These personal, localized gestures of support may matter more for overall clergy well-being than many of the formal, large-scale ways in which clergy experience care.[3] However, these more formal structures care for clergy en masse, have broader impact, and are the subject of our inquiry.

Initially, we selected four critical sectors in the network of those providing care for clergy. Those sectors were (1) denominations, networks, and associations; (2) pension, benefit, and insurance providers; (3) granting organizations and funders; and (4) frontline providers. The fifth sector—continuing education providers—was recommended by Jo Ann Deasy of ATS. She said that often when a clergyperson reaches a dry point in their ministry, their first call is not to someone in their denominational network, a licensed therapist, or a coach. Instead, their first call is often to a seminary to sign up for a doctor of ministry or other continuing education programing. She noted that these clergy hope that more education will help them grow in their ministry and fix some of the underlying problems they might face. As a result of her recommendation, we decided to include a fifth sector called continuing education providers, which includes all providers of education to pastors beyond their initial seminary degree or theological training.

Our recruitment strategy included four distinct phases. First, we reached out to professional associations within each of the sectors we identified. For instance, in the continuing education sector, we partnered with ATS, the Association of Leaders in Lifelong Learning in Ministry (ALLLM), and the Association of Doctor of Ministry Education Professionals (ADME). For the pension, benefit, and insurance sector, we partnered with members of the Church Benefits Association (CBA) and major for-profit firms like Brotherhood Mutual and Church Mutual.

Representatives from professional associations, many of whom served on our advisory board, contacted their networks, inviting their respective

---

3. We also acknowledge that these more localized expressions of support are especially important in minority communities where large-scale structures may not exist or may not exist in the same way as those established within majority communities. See ch. 2 for more details.

constituencies to participate in our survey. In other cases, our team extended personal invitations for members of the field to participate in the survey, often scheduling one-on-one calls to inform potential participants about the project and invite their participation.

The second phase in the research design was to determine the survey questions. In addition to looking at other surveys of clergy and congregations, we recorded interviews with our advisory board to understand the greatest challenges and nagging questions they face in their work day-to-day. We analyzed the transcripts and developed survey questions based on the themes we discovered. Specifically, we focused our questions on the organization of the network of clergy care providers, the activity that they undertake, and the way providers conceptualize both their work and their place in the network. Upon developing these survey questions, our academic advisors reviewed them for consistency with survey methodology and their own expertise. We submitted the survey to the Duke Clinical and Translational Science Institute for a plain-language consultation to ensure that the language we used was both clear and accessible to a broad audience. Then, our professional advisors tested the survey to be sure that the survey mechanism worked correctly and to be sure that the questions were properly phrased (see appendix B for our survey).

Third, we launched the survey in June 2021, and it remained open through March 2022. Initially, we did not have high expectations for the survey since we had launched it in the middle of the pandemic and during the first summer of renewed travel after the COVID-19 lockdowns in 2020. On average, participants completed the survey within twenty to thirty minutes. Despite these hurdles, we achieved a 50 percent response rate. This speaks to the energy in the field to engage in this work and connect with each other. We received many notes of gratitude and appreciation that someone was interested in the work of our participants. Our final response rate was 47 percent. We initially excluded retreat centers from our outreach during the summer since they were involved with summer programming, the first in two years. Following outreach to the retreat centers in October 2021, the response rate dropped from 50 percent to 47 percent.

In addition to survey data, we collected qualitative data from interviews and focus groups conducted during 2021–2022. These interviews and focus groups were primarily conducted with people who had taken our survey. We used these focus groups to further illuminate the themes and findings we saw in the survey data. Our participants added further clarity and refinement to our findings. Our focus groups drew on the responses provided by our participants in their surveys. For instance, one focus group addressed the resistance clergy caregivers face in their ministry. To explore this topic, we randomly selected a group of providers from our survey participants who had experienced resistance in providing care to clergy. For the interviews, we intentionally selected our participants because these persons represent major themes we see emerging from the data, types of services provided, or populations served.

Coding and analysis of survey data, the fourth phase, began in August 2021 and continued until the survey was closed. Quantitative survey data was cleaned to allow for greater ease in the analysis. Many of the key variables were binary, and we began with cross-tabulations to assess whether the variables were associated with each other. We then used logistic regression analysis to assess statistical significance.

We made several site visits and conducted in-depth case studies on the themes of supporting women and bivocational clergy, retreat centers, socio-cultural context, spirituality, and well-being. The first case study was of a retreat center in the southwestern United States. The host, a woman with pastoral experience and the daughter of a pastor, started the retreat center as a way to help clergy reconnect and recover from the challenges of ministry. The retreat center provides various forms of evidence-based therapy, physical activity, and fellowship among colleagues.

The second case study also involved a retreat, but it was with a cohort of women clergy. The hosts had received funding for many years to sponsor a cohort of women clergy. The women apply to be in a cohort and commit to several years of virtual and in-person meetings. The hosts' goal was to provide a space for women clergy to find support and support each other.

The final case study involved a denominational official who cared for bivocational clergy in the central United States. This case study explored the challenges that he contended with in caring for an underserved population (lack of resources, lack of accessibility). The denominational official shared about the needs that he addressed in his work such as financial compensation, rest, and education. Each case study illuminated some key themes in the research and the people involved in doing the hard work of caring for clergy.

Similar to the qualitative interviews and focus groups, these case studies illuminated themes found in the survey data. They also gave us insight on the practice of clergy caregiving. During site visits, we gathered ethnographic data on how clergy caregivers coordinated their services and programs, how they stayed motivated, interacted with clergy, and managed the challenges of clergy caregiving. We observed and participated in clergy retreats in the Midwest, Southwest, and Pacific Northwest. One was composed of mainline clergy, one was composed of evangelical clergy, and one was composed of a mixture of clergy from various denominational backgrounds.

Additionally, we collected IRS Form 990s for foundations who issued grants containing the terms "clergy," "pastor," or "minister" from 2003 to 2019.[4] We manually coded the resulting 3,981 grants for whether or not they addressed clergy care and whether that care directly benefited clergy or indirectly benefited them by helping them to more effectively perform their ministry. This source of data provided additional information on the resources made available for clergy care and how those resources have fluctuated over the past two decades.

4. For a similar methodology, see Lindsay and Wuthnow, "Financing Faith."

Appendix B

Survey

Introduction

Q2.1   What is the name of your organization or practice?

Q2.2   Please describe your denomination or church affiliation and/ or theological tradition. Use as many descriptors as you feel are needed for the researchers to understand your tradition.
For example: non-denominational, Pentecostal, Black church; Mainline, United Methodist, etc.

Q2.3   What is the website for your organization or practice?

Q2.4   What is your name?

Q2.5   What is your email address?

Let's Get Started! Continued

Q3.1   What best describes your primary organization or practice? Select ALL that apply:

- Denomination, network, or association
- Single congregation

- Pension, benefit, or insurance organization serving clergy/pastors
- Granting organization funding services and programs for clergy/pastors
- Retreat center welcoming clergy/pastors
- Counseling practice or center caring for clergy/pastors
- Continuing education practice providing services for clergy/pastors
- Resource center for clergy/pastors
- Social work practice caring for clergy/pastors
- Seminary
- Other: please explain. _____

Q3.2 Does your organization or practice currently offer services that care for or serve clergy/pastors? Please choose the best option below (only one selection is possible).

- Yes, directly
- Yes, but indirectly as a foundation or philanthropic partner
- No
- Other: please explain. _____

Q3.3 Does your pension, benefit, or insurance organization give grants for clergy or pastor care?

- Yes
- No

Q3.4 In the past, did your organization or practice provide services or programs that cared for or served clergy/pastors?

- Yes
- No

Q3.5 What was the reason (or reasons) for ending these services or programs offered to clergy/pastors?

- List reasons _____
- I do not know

Q3.6 Does your organization intend to develop new initiatives to care for or serve clergy/pastors in the next one to three years?

- Yes
- No
- I do not know

Q3.7 Are you responsible for overseeing, leading, implementing, or advising programs or services caring for or serving clergy/pastors for your organization or practice?

- Yes
- No

Q3.8 Does your work have either a direct or indirect effect on programs/services available to clergy?

- Yes
- No

Q3.9 Can you refer us to a person in your organization (or another organization) who does have responsibility in overseeing, leading, or implementing programs or services caring for or serving clergy/pastors? Thank you!

- Yes
- No

Q3.10 Please provide the referral information below. Thank you.

Name _____

Position/title _____

Email address _____

Q3.11 How many clergy/pastors are part of your overall organization or practice? Approximate estimates are okay.

Number of clergy/pastors: _____

I do not know.

Q3.12 In the twelve months pre-COVID, how many clergy/pastors used your services or programs? Approximate estimates are okay.

Number of clergy/pastors: _____

I do not know.

Q3.13 How many clergy/pastors use your services over a twelve-month period? Approximate estimates are okay.

Number of clergy/pastors: _____

I do not know.

Let's Talk about the Reach of Your Work

Q4.1 Which best describes your organization or practice? Note: Select the broadest category that applies

- An international organization
- A national organization
- A regional organization
- A local organization

Q4.2 Please select the region, or regions, that best describes the geographical area where your organization works. Check ALL that apply.

- Southeast: (FL, MS, AL, GA, SC, NC, VA, KY, TN, WV)
- Northeast: (DC, DE, MD, PA, NY, NJ, RI, MA, CT, ME, NH, VT)
- Midwest: (OH, IN, MI, IL WI, MN, IA, ND, SD)
- South Central: (TX, LA, AR, MO, NE, KS, OH, NM)

- Southwest: (CA, NV, UT, CO, AZ, HI)

- Pacific Northwest: (WA, OR, ID, MT, WY)

- Outside of the continental USA. Please name the area or areas, e.g., HI, AK, US Territory, etc.: _____

- Other: please list and/or explain.

Q4.3   If your organization is local, please provide the following information:

Name of the city or town where you are located _____

State _____

Zip code _____

Tell Us about Your Organization/Practice

Q5.1   What is your organization's total annual budget? Approximate numbers are OK.

Q5.2   What is the age of your organization or practice?

- Less than 1 year

- 1–5 years

- 6–10 years

- 11–20 years

- More than 20 years old

Q5.3   How long has your organization provided services or programs that care for or serve clergy/pastors?

- Less than 1 year

- 1–5 years

- 6–10 years

- 11–20 years

- More than 20 years

Tell Us about Your Role!

Q6.1   What is your job title within your organization or practice?

Q6.2   Is the primary function of your position to care for or serve clergy/pastors?

- Yes, full-time
- No, part-time

Q6.3   During a typical work week how much of your time is devoted to caring for or serving clergy/pastors?

- 0–5 hours
- 6–10 hours
- 11–20 hours
- 20+ hours

Q6.4   What other responsibilities do you have in your job besides caring for clergy/pastors? Please list.

Q6.5   How many years have you been in your role of caring for or serving clergy/pastors?

- 0–5
- 6–10
- 11–15
- 16–20
- 21–25
- 25+

Q6.6   Have you ever served a local congregation in pastoral ministry yourself?

- Yes
- No

Q6.7 Please state how much you agree/disagree with the following statement: "I believe that God has called me to care for clergy/pastors as part of my vocation."

- Strongly agree
- Somewhat agree
- Neither agree nor disagree
- Somewhat disagree
- Strongly disagree

Tell Us about Your Goals and Insights!

Q7.1 When thinking about the care or service you provide to clergy/pastors, what formal goals does your organization have? (Include whether these goals are short-term or long-term).

- If you do have formal goals, please list the goals: _____
  _____
- No formal goals have been set.

Q7.2 In the past twelve months has your organization or practice undertaken a formal process seeking feedback from the clergy/pastors you serve to learn if you are meeting their felt needs?

- Yes
- No

Q7.3 What were the greatest insights you heard from clergy/pastors? List up to three.

- First insight: _____
- Second insight: _____
- Third insight: _____

Tell Us about the Care You Provide!

Q8.1   In which of the following areas does your organization or practice care for or serve clergy/pastors? Select ALL that apply.

- Mental/emotional heath

- Bodily/physical health

- Spiritual formation

- Marriage

- Parenting

- Caring for aging parents

- Personal social life

- Culture and/or societal issues

- Financial literacy

- Financial/material well-being

- The relationship between clergy/pastors and their congregation

- The relationship between clergy/pastors and their denomination or church organization

- Other: please describe. _____

Q8.2   Do you have formal training, certification, and/or credentials for the services or programs your organization provides for clergy/pastors?

- Yes

- No

Q8.3   What formal training, certification, and/or credentials do you personally have for the services or programs your organization provides for clergy/pastors? Please provide the credential you received and the name of the granting institution.

Q8.4   Do you have informal training for the services or programs your organization provides for clergy/pastors?

- Yes

- No

Q8.5   Please describe any informal training or experiences you have had that supports your work caring for or serving clergy/pastors.

Q8.6   Does your organization have a definition of clergy/pastor well-being?

- Yes

- No

Q8.7   What is the definition? Please write the definition in the box below.

Q8.8   What concepts, values, or ideas do you think are important to include in a definition of clergy well-being?

What Do Others Think?

Q9.1   Within your organization or practice, do you experience resistance to prioritizing programs or services that care for or serve clergy/ pastors?

- Yes

- No

Q9.2   Where do you perceive the resistance coming from? Select ALL that apply:

- Denominational officials

- Clergy

- Lay leaders

- Congregations

- Lack of funding

- Lack of time/competing responsibilities

- Other: _____

Q9.3   What is a primary reason for the resistance?

- Please explain. _____

- I don't know.

Q9.4   What have you found helpful or effective in convincing others in your organization or practice of the importance of caring for or serving clergy/pastors?

How Do You Do Your Work?

Q10.1   What is the source of funding that enables your organization to care for or serve clergy/pastors? Check ALL that apply.

- Grants
- Endowment(s)
- Fee for service
- General budget of a local congregation
- Denominational support
- Individual/major donor(s)
- Other source: please explain. _____

Q10.2   In an earlier question you provided budget information about your overall organization. This question focuses on the specific budget you have to care for or serve clergy/pastors. What is the annual budget allocated for programs or services for clergy/pastors?

- $0 (I do not have a budget)
- $1–$50,000
- $50,001–$100,000
- $100,001–$500,000
- $500,001–$999,999
- $1 million–$50 million
- $50 million–$100 million
- More than $100 million

Q10.3   Do you feel that this budget allocation is enough for the programs/services you want or need to provide?

- Yes
- No

Q10.4   What is your best estimate of the amount of grant funding that you award for clergy/pastor care per year?

Q10.5   What is the average size ($) of the grants you give for clergy/pastor care?

- $0–$10,000
- $10,001–$50,000
- $50,001–$100,000
- More than $100,000

Q10.6   Does your organization or practice have any of the following initiatives to support or care for clergy/pastors? Select ALL that apply.

- Job descriptions with expectations related to clergy well-being
- Personnel policies for clergy/pastors specifically related to maintaining health and well-being
- Sabbaticals for clergy/pastors
- A structure or program for congregations/lay leaders to check on and care for clergy/pastors
- A structure or program for the denomination or association to check on and care for clergy/pastors
- Guaranteed/minimum salary for clergy/pastors
- A retirement plan
- Health insurance
- Retreat facilities for clergy/pastors
- Counseling and/or mental health services
- Training for diversity and inclusion
- Programs or services supporting equality and or/racial justice
- Programs or services supporting clergy/pastors' families and marriages
- Programs helping clergy/pastors understand and deal with the impacts of poverty, injustice, polarization, or socio-cultural incidents (e.g., riots, terrorist attacks, etc.)

- In-depth evaluation of clergy candidates in the ordination process
- Executive leadership and wellness coaching
- Spiritual direction
- Financial management consulting
- Church and clergy/pastor discipline processes
- Conflict resolution and assertiveness training
- Continuing education opportunities
- Other initiatives (please list)

Tell Us about Your Programs/Services

Q11.1   Please list the names or titles of up to four services or programs that your organization or practice provides that care for or serve clergy/pastors. Please include a short description and/or any web page links, if applicable.

Q11.2   What problem and/or root causes are these services/programs attempting to solve? Please describe.

Q11.3   Clergy care programs and services are probably a mixture of both prevention and treatment. Do any of the activities you listed above focus primarily on prevention as opposed to treatment? Select ALL that apply.

Q11.4   From your perspective are any of your programs listed above especially innovative? If so, select ALL that apply.

Q11.5   From your perspective are any of your programs listed above especially effective? If so, select ALL that apply.

Q11.6   From your perspective are any of your programs listed above especially scalable? If so, select ALL that apply.

Q11.7   Which program or service is most popularly used by clergy/pastors?

Q11.8 From your perspective what is one of the greatest challenges you face delivering services or programs that care for or serve clergy/pastors?

Q11.9 For whom do you offer services/programs? Select ALL that apply.

- Full-time clergy/pastors
- Part-time clergy/pastors
- Bivocational clergy/pastors

Q11.10 How many grants per year do you award for programs/services that support or care for clergy/pastors?

- 0–25
- 26–100
- 100+

Q11.11 How many grants per year do you award for RESEARCH that supports clergy/pastor care?

- 0–25
- 26–100
- 100+

How Do You Serve Those in Need?

Q12.1 Based on your knowledge of your organization or practice, please respond to the following statement: My organization's/practice's programs and services are inclusive and intentionally REACHING racial minority clergy/pastors (e.g., Black, Latinx, etc.).

- Strongly agree
- Somewhat agree
- Neither agree nor disagree
- Somewhat disagree
- Strongly disagree

Q12.2   Based on your knowledge of your organization or practice, please respond to the following statement: My organization's/practice's programs and services are EFFECTIVE at meeting the needs of racial minority clergy/pastors (e.g., Black, Latinx, etc.).

- Strongly agree
- Somewhat agree
- Neither agree nor disagree
- Somewhat disagree
- Strongly disagree

Q12.3   Based on your knowledge of your organization or practice, please respond to the following statement: My organization's/practice's programs and services are inclusive and intentionally REACHING women clergy/pastors.

- Strongly agree
- Somewhat agree
- Neither agree nor disagree
- Somewhat disagree
- Strongly disagree

Q12.4   Based on your knowledge of your organization or practice, please respond to the following statement: My organization's/practice's programs and services are EFFECTIVE at meeting the needs of women clergy/pastors.

- Strongly agree
- Somewhat agree
- Neither agree nor disagree
- Somewhat disagree
- Strongly disagree

Q12.5   Has your organization continued or started any new programs in the past two years specifically to help clergy/pastors respond to the recent racial conflicts in American society and culture?

- Yes
- No

Q12.6   Has your organization continued or started any new programs in the past two years specifically to help clergy/pastors address racism in the church?

- Yes
- No

Q12.7 Has your organization continued or started any new programs in the past two years specifically to help clergy/pastors address sexism in the church?

- Yes
- No

Q12.8   Has your organization continued or started any new programs specifically to help clergy/pastors respond to the recent impacts and stress due to COVID-19?

- Yes
- No

Tell Us about Your Inspirations!

Q13.1   From your perspective what are the new frontiers, or big opportunities, for advancing the field caring for or serving clergy/pastors?

Q13.2   What books, articles, and/or literature do you draw on in your work? List the top three, if applicable.

- Title #1 _____
- Author #1 (if known) _____
- Title #2 _____
- Author #2 (if known) _____

- Title #3 _____
- Author #3 (if known) _____

Q13.3 Who or what is inspiring you in your work (e.g., authors, thought leaders, programs, resources, etc.)? List up to three.

- Inspiration #1 _____
- Inspiration #2 _____
- Inspiration #3 _____

Q13.4 Do you collaborate with other organizations in your work?

- Yes
- No

Q13.5 Who do you collaborate with? Please list the names of up to four partner organizations or networks below.

- Organization/Network 1 _____
- Organization/Network 2 _____
- Organization/Network 3 _____
- Organization/Network 4 _____

Q13.6 Do you (or does your organization/practice) belong to any of the following professional associations? Select ALL that apply

- Association of Doctor of Ministry Directors
- Association for Hispanic Theological Education (AETH)
- Association of Leaders in Lifelong Learning for Ministry (ALLLM)
- Association of Related Churches (ARC)
- Association of Theological Schools
- Caregivers Forum
- Church Alliance
- Church Benefits Association
- Christian Camp & Conference Association
- Christian Church Together

- Ecumenical Stewardship Center
- Full Strength Network
- Ministers Fellowship International
- National Association of United Methodist Foundations
- Professionals in Christian Philanthropy
- The Gathering
- The Episcopal Network for Stewardship
- Wesleyan Church Thriving Clergy Care Coordinators
- Not applicable
- Others (please list): _____

Q13.7 Would you be interested in exploring further partnerships with other organizations?

- Yes
- No

Three Last Questions . . .

Q14.1 May our research team follow up with you for further conversation about your responses, if needed?

- Yes
- No

Q14.2 May our team contact you with our research findings and/or about future studies?

- Yes
- No

Q14.3 Is there anything else you would like to share with us?

Bibliography

Adams, Jimi. "Stained Glass Makes the Ceiling Visible: Organizational Opposition to Women in Congregational Leadership." *Gender and Society* 21, no. 1 (2007) 80–105.

Action Alliance. "Resource." Action Alliance, n.d. https://theactionalliance.org/faith-hope-life/american-association-pastoral-counselors.

Adams, Jay E. *Competent to Counsel: Introduction to Nouthetic Counseling.* Grand Rapids: Ministry Resources Library, 1970.

Albritton, Travis J. "Educating Our Own: The Historical Legacy of HBCUs and Their Relevance for Educating a New Generation of Leaders." *Urban Review* 44, no. 3 (2012) 311–31. https://doi.org/10.1007/s11256-012-0202-9.

American Hospital Association. "Medical Students Form Maine COVID Sitters to Support Health Care Heroes." American Hospital Association, May 20, 2020. https://www.aha.org/other-resources/2020-05-20-medical-students-form-maine-covid-sitters-support-health-care-heroes.

Anderson, Javonte. "Closed Doors, Virtual Services and Lawsuits: Here's How the Pandemic Has Affected Religion in Chicagoland." *Chicago Tribune*, September 13, 2020. https://www.chicagotribune.com/news/breaking/ct-coronavirus-chicago-religion-six-pandemic-months-20200913-feqhwoncbvba3nl3xervec2joy-story.html.

Andrews, Valerie. "Designing a Program to Help Urban Pastors Cope With Compassion Stress." PhD diss., Thomas Jefferson University, 2021.

Ankel, Sophia. "Pastors Are Leaving Their Congregations after Losing Their Churchgoers to QAnon." *Business Insider*, March 14, 2021. https://www.businessinsider.com/pastors-quit-after-qanon-radicalize-congregation-2021-3.

Association for Doctor of Ministry Education. "History." DMin Education, 2022. https://dmineducation.org/history/.

Association of Related Churches. https://www.arcchurches.com/about/.

Austin, Thad S. *Giving USA Special Report: Giving to Religion.* Indianapolis: Giving USA Foundation, 2017.

Baines, Donna. "Race, Resistance, and Restructuring: Emerging Skills in the New Social Services." *Social Work* 53, no. 2 (2008) 123–31.

Baker, Wayne. "Oldest African American Seminary in U.S. Continues during Pandemic." *Dayton Daily News*, updated May 17, 2020. https://www.daytondailynews.com/news/local-education/oldest-african-american-seminary-continues-during-pandemic/MXXUNoIpfRsymDXhopiOEO/.

Banks, Adelle. "Black Seminary Grads, with Debt Higher than Others, Cope with Money and Ministry." *Religion News Service*, February 17, 2022. https://religionnews.com/2022/02/17/black-seminary-grads-with-debt-higher-than-others-cope-with-money-and-ministry/.

Barna Group. "38% of U.S. Pastors Have Thought about Quitting Full-Time Ministry in the Past Year." Barna, November 16, 2021. https://www.barna.com/research/pastors-well-being/.

Baruth, Megan, et al. "The Health and Health Behaviors of a Sample of African American Pastors." *Journal of Health Care for the Poor and Underserved* 25, no. 1 (2014) 229–41. https://doi.org/10.1353/hpu.2014.0041.

Bekkers, René, and Pamala Wiepking. "Who Gives? A Literature Review of Predictors of Charitable Giving Part One: Religion, Education, Age and Socialisation." *Voluntary Sector Review* 2, no. 3 (2011) 337–65. https://doi.org/10.1332/204080511X6087712.

Bevins, Winfield, and Mark Dunwoody. *Healthy Rhythms for Leaders: Cultivating Soul Care in Uncertain Times.* Chicago: Exponential, 2021.

Blair, Leonardo. "AME Church Will No Longer Allow 'One Person to Count the Money' after Nearly $100M Goes Missing." *Christian Post*, March 25, 2022. https://www.christianpost.com/news/ame-church-sued-after-100m-goes-missing.html.

Blair, Samuel. *An Account of the College of New-Jersey.* Woodbridge, NJ: Parker, 1764.

Bloom, Matt. "Burning Out in Ministry: Research Insights from the Flourishing in Ministry Project." Work Well Research, July 2017. https://workwellresearch.org/wp-content/uploads/2019/11/FIM_Report_Burnout2.pdf.

———. *Flourishing in Ministry: How to Cultivate Clergy Well-Being.* Lanham, MD: Rowman & Littlefield, 2019.

Board of Pensions of the Presbyterian Church (U.S.A.), The. "Our History." Board of Pensions, n.d. https://pensions.org/our-role-and-purpose/about-us/our-history. Accessed May 21, 2022.

Boigegrain, Barbara. "Fall 2010 GBHEM Board Meeting." YouTube, October 13, 2010. https://www.youtube.com/watch?v=YS8gXGyCU8w.

Bradley, David Henry. *A History of the A. M. E. Zion Church, Part 2: 1872–1968.* Eugene, OR: Wipf and Stock, 2020.

Bradshaw, Paul F. *Rites of Ordination: Their History and Theology.* Collegeville, MN: Liturgical, 2013.

Brotherhood Mutual. "Bearing One Another's Burdens." Brotherhood Mutual, n.d. http://www.brotherhoodmutual.com/about-us/100-years/. Accessed May 5, 2022.

———. "Brotherhood Mutual Donates $500,000 to Full Strength Network." Brotherhood Mutual, November 10, 2020. http://www.brotherhoodmutual.com/news-media-center/brotherhood-mutual-donates-500-000-to-full-strength-network/.

———. "Who We Are." Brotherhood Mutual, n.d. http://www.brotherhoodmutual.com/about-us/who-we-are/. Accessed May 5, 2022.

Brown, Jessica Young. "Jessica Young Brown: Ministers Cannot Thrive If They Neglect Themselves." *Faith and Leadership*, May 12, 2020. https://faithandleadership.com/jessica-young-brown-ministers-cannot-thrive-if-they-neglect-themselves.

Brown, Kenneth O. "Finding America's Oldest Camp Meeting." *Methodist History* 28, no. 4 (July 1990) 252–53.

Brown, Olu. *A New Kind of Venture Leader.* Greatest Expedition 6. Knoxville: Market Square, 2021.

Brubacher, J. S., and W. Rudy. *Higher Education in Transition: A History of American Colleges and Universities.* New York: Transaction, 1997.

Bumgardner, David. "They Spoke Out against the Capitol Insurrection; One Year Later, They're No Longer Pastors." *Baptist News Global,* January 19, 2022. https://baptistnews.com/article/they-spoke-out-against-the-capitol-insurrection-one-year-later-theyre-no-longer-pastors/.

Burns, Bob, et al. *The Politics of Ministry: Navigating Power Dynamics and Negotiating Interests.* Downers Grove, IL: InterVarsity, 2019.

Cafferata, Gail. "Gender, Judicatory Respect and Pastors' Well-Being in Closing Churches." *Review of Religious Research* 62, no. 2 (2020) 369–87. https://doi.org/10.1007/s13644-020-00414-1.

CareGivers Forum. "Directory of Ministries." CareGivers Forum, n.d. https://www.caregiversforum.org/directory.

———. "The History of CareGivers Forum." CareGivers Forum, n.d. https://www.caregiversforum.org/history.

Carnegie Corporation of New York. "The Origins of the Carnegie Foundation for the Advancement of Teaching and the Birth of TIAA-CREF." Carnegie Corporation, May 7, 2015. https://www.carnegie.org/news/articles/origins-carnegie-foundation-advancement-teaching-and-birth-tiaa-cref/.

Carroll, Jackson W. *God's Potters: Pastoral Leadership and the Shaping of Congregations.* Grand Rapids: Eerdmans, 2006.

———. "Toward 2000: Some Futures for Religious Leadership." *Review of Religious Research* 33, no. 4 (1992) 289–304. https://doi.org/10.2307/3511602.

Carson, Kevin. "When a Pastor Commits Suicide . . . a Letter to the Church." Kevin Carson (blog), May 9, 2020. https://kevincarson.com/2020/05/09/when-a-pastor-commits-suicide-a-letter-to-the-church/.

Cebula, Judith. "Thriving in Ministry Grants to Help Pastors in Congregational Ministry." Lilly Endowment, October 1, 2018. https://lillyendowment.org/news/thriving-in-ministry-grants-to-help-pastors-in-congregational-ministry/.

Chaves, Mark. *Congregations in America.* Cambridge, MA: Harvard University Press, 2009.

———, et al. *Congregations in 21st Century America.* Durham, NC: Duke University, Department of Sociology, 2021. https://sites.duke.edu/ncsweb/files/2022/02/NCSIV_Report_Web_FINAL2.pdf.

Cherry, Conrad. *Hurrying toward Zion: Universities, Divinity Schools, and American Protestantism.* Bloomington: Indiana University Press, 1995.

Chopp, Rebecca. Review of *Theologia: The Fragmentation and Unity of Theological Education,* by Edward Farley. *Journal of Religion* 65, no. 2 (1985) 296–98.

Christian Camp & Conference Association. "Vision—Mission—Values." Christian Camp & Conference Association, n.d. https://www.ccca.org/ccca/Vision,_Mission,_Values.asp. Accessed April 14, 2022.

Christian Church Foundation. https://www.christianchurchfoundation.org/about-intro.

Christian Methodist Episcopal Church General Board of Personnel Services. "The General Board of Personnel Services." GBPS, n.d. http://www.gbpsonline.org/. Accessed April 11, 2022.

Chung-Kim, Esther. *Economics of Faith: Reforming Poverty in Early Modern Europe.* Oxford Studies in Historical Theology Series. New York: Oxford University Press, 2021. https://doi.org/10.1093/oso/9780197537732.001.0001.

Church Benefits Association. https://www.churchbenefitsassociation.org.

Church Mutual Insurance Company. "About Us: Company History." Church Mutual Insurance Company, 2022. https://www.churchmutual.com/87/Company-History.

Church Pension Fund. "Statement of the Board of Trustees as to Retirement Age." April 27, 1956.

Church Pension Group. "About CREDO." Church Pension Group, n.d. https://www.cpg.org/active-clergy/learning/credo/about-credo/. Accessed May 9, 2022.

COGIC Urban Initiatives, Inc. "Grant Opportunities in Response to the COVID-19 Crisis." COGIC Urban Initiatives, Inc., n.d. https://www.cogic.org/urbaninitiatives/files/2020/04/CUI-Grant-Opportunties-In-Response-to-COVID-19.pdf.

Collins, Gary R. *Christian Coaching: Helping Others Turn Potential into Reality.* Colorado Springs, CO: NavPress, 2001.

———. *Christian Counseling: A Comprehensive Guide.* Waco, TX: Word, 1980.

Comsikey, Joel. *You Can Coach: How to Help Leaders Build Healthy Churches through Coaching.* Moreno Valley, CA: CCS, 2010.

Common Table Collaborative. https://commontable.network.

Cross, F. L., and Elizabeth A. Livingstone, eds. "Seminary." In *The Oxford Dictionary of the Christian Church*, 1491. Oxford, UK: Oxford University Press, 2005.

Davies, Glenn N. "Sacrifice, Offerings, Gifts." In *Dictionary of the Later New Testament and Its Developments*, edited by Ralph P. Martin and Peter H. Davids, 1071. Downers Grove, IL: InterVarsity, 1997.

Davis, James D. "Black Clergy to Get Some Tips on Foundation Grants." *Sun Sentinel*, July 26, 1997. https://www.sun-sentinel.com/news/fl-xpm-1997-07-26-9707240406-story.html.

Davis, Jonathan. "If You Are a Pastor in an Abusive Church, Please Know That You Are Not Alone." *Baptist News Global*, August 23, 2021. https://baptistnews.com/article/if-you-are-a-pastor-in-an-abusive-church-please-know-that-you-are-not-alone/.

Dawson, Tracey. "Whose Problem Is Clergy Burnout?" *Christian Century*, November 5, 2020. https://www.christiancentury.org/article/recommendations/whose-problem-clergy-burnout.

Deasy, Jo Ann. "Graduating Student Questionnaire Reveals Fewer Students Taking Out Loans and Other Insights." *Association of Theological Schools*, October 2017. https://www.ats.edu/files/galleries/gsq-reveals-fewer-students-taking-out-loans.pdf.

Debuchy, Paul. "Retreats." In vol. 12 of *The Catholic Encyclopedia*. New York: Appleton, 1911. https://www.newadvent.org/cathen/12795b.htm.

Department of Retirement Services. "Important Update on AMEC Retirement Services." AME Church, March 31, 2022. https://www.ame-church.com/news/important-update-on-amec-retirement-services/.

Douyon, Emmanuela, and Alyssa Sepinwall. "Earthquakes and Storms Are Natural, but Haiti's Disasters Are Man-Made, Too." *Washington Post*, August 20, 2021. https://

www.washingtonpost.com/outlook/2021/08/20/earthquakes-storms-are-natural-haitis-disasters-are-man-made-too/.

Duke Endowment. "Rural Church." Duke Endowment, n.d. https://www.dukeendowment. org/our-work/rural-church. Accessed May 24, 2022.

Duke Global Health Institute. "Duke Clergy Health Initiative." Duke Global Health Institute, n.d. https://globalhealth.duke.edu/projects/duke-clergy-health-initiative. Accessed April 20, 2022.

Duke, James B. "Indenture of Trust." Duke Endowment, December 11, 1924. https://www. dukeendowment.org/uploads/resource-library/Duke-Endowmennt-Indenture-of-Trust.pdf.

Eagle, David, et al. "Seminary to Early Ministry." Presentation for the Duke Endowment, December 2020.

Earls, Aaron. "Few Pastors Left the Pulpit Despite Increased Pressure." Lifeway Research, October 25, 2021. https://research.lifeway.com/2021/10/25/few-pastors-left-the-pulpit-despite-increased-pressure/.

Eastwood, Cyril. *The Priesthood of All Believers: An Examination of the Doctrine from the Reformation to the Present Day.* Eugene, OR: Wipf and Stock, 2009.

Ecumenical Stewardship Center. https://web.archive.org/web/20201127024242/https:// stewardshipresources.org/about/.

ECFPL. "The Coordination Program." ECFPL, n.d. https://www.ecfpl.org/.

Edwards, Laura, et al. "The Relationship between Social Support, Spiritual Well-Being, and Depression in Christian Clergy: A Systematic Literature Review." *Mental Health, Religion & Culture* 23, no. 10 (2020) 857–73.

Eliot, John. *New Englands* [sic] *First Fruits.* London: Printed by R. O. and G. D. [R. Oulton and G. Dexter] for Henry Overton, 1643.

Elliott, Justin, and Laura Sullivan. "How the Red Cross Raised Half a Billion Dollars for Haiti and Built Six Homes." *ProPublica*, June 3, 2015. https://www.propublica. org/article/how-the-red-cross-raised-half-a-billion-dollars-for-haiti-and-built-6-homes?token=3-02TVyAqASwdG65PPRjM0V-pxKrSOzK.

Elliott, T. G. "The Tax Exemptions Granted to Clerics by Constantine and Constantius II." *Phoenix* 32, no. 4 (1978) 326–36. https://doi.org/10.2307/1087959.

Elwell, Walter A., and Philip Wesley Comfort. *Tyndale Bible Dictionary.* Wheaton, IL: Tyndale, 2001.

Episcopal Church Foundation. https://www.ecf.org/about.

Evans, Craig A., and Stanley E. Porter Jr, eds. *Dictionary of New Testament Background: A Compendium of Contemporary Biblical Scholarship.* Downers Grove, IL: InterVarsity, 2000.

Farley, Edward. *Theologia: The Fragmentation and Unity of Theological Education.* Eugene, OR: Wipf and Stock, 2001.

Faulkner, John Alfred. *The Methodists.* Charlotte, NC: Baker & Taylor, 1903.

Ferguson, Sinclair B., et al. *New Dictionary of Theology.* Downers Grove, IL: InterVarsity, 2000.

Florer-Bixler, Melissa. "Why Pastors Are Joining the Great Resignation." *Sojourners*, November 30, 2021. https://sojo.net/articles/why-pastors-are-joining-great-resignation.

Francis, Leslie J., et al. "Assessing Clergy Work-Related Psychological Health: Reliability and Validity of the Francis Burnout Inventory." *Mental Health, Religion & Culture* 20, no. 9 (2017) 911–21. https://doi.org/10.1080/13674676.2017.1373333.

Full Strength Network. https://fullstrength.org/about/.

Fulton, Brad R. "26. Religious Organizations: Crosscutting the Nonprofit Sector." In *The Nonprofit Sector: A Research Handbook*, 3rd ed., edited by Walter W. Powell and Patricia Bromley, 579–98. Redwood City, CA: Stanford University Press, 2020. https://doi.org/10.1515/9781503611085-035.

Gamble, Connolly C. "Continuing Education for Ministry—Perspectives and Prospects." Society for the Advancement of Continuing Education for Ministry, June 16, 1975. Annual meeting speech transcript, 11.

———. *The Continuing Theological Education of the American Minister*. Richmond, VA: Union Theological Seminary, 1960.

Gawain, Shakti. *The Four Levels of Healing: A Guide to Balancing the Spiritual, Mental, Emotional, and Physical Aspects of Life*. Mill Valley, CA: Nataraj, 1997.

Geiger, R. L. *The History of American Higher Education: Learning and Culture from the Founding to World War II*. Princeton, NJ: Princeton University Press, 2014.

General Board of Pension and Health Benefits of the United Methodist Church. *A Century of Caring, Continuing to Serve*. 2008.

Goodstein, Laurie. "Early Alarm for Church on Abusers in the Clergy." *New York Times*, April 2, 2009. https://www.nytimes.com/2009/04/03/us/03church.html?_r=1&hpw.

Gorny, Nicki. "Christ the King Pastor Resigns, Citing Vocation." *Yahoo News*, August 22, 2021. https://news.yahoo.com/christ-king-pastor-resigns-citing-030500139.html.

Goswami, Chris. "How Did a Gifted Christian Minister Become an Atheist? I Met Him to Find Out." *Premier Christianity*, April 5, 2022. https://www.premierchristianity.com/apologetics/how-did-a-gifted-christian-minister-become-an-atheist-i-met-him-to-find-out/12805.article.

Green, Joel B., and L. Hurst. "Priest, Priesthood." In *Dictionary of Jesus and the Gospels*, edited by Joel B. Green et al., 634. Downers Grove, IL: InterVarsity, 1992.

Green, Lisa Cannon. "Despite Stresses, Few Pastors Give Up on Ministry." Lifeway Research, September 1, 2015. https://research.lifeway.com/2015/09/01/despite-stresses-few-pastors-give-up-on-ministry/.

Hands, Donald R., and Wayne L. Fehr. *Spiritual Wholeness for Clergy: A New Psychology of Intimacy with God, Self, and Others*. Washington, DC: Alban Institute, 1993.

H. E. Butt Foundation. "Job Description." H. E. Butt Foundation, February 2022. https://hebfdn.org/wp-content/uploads/sites/7/2022/02/Executive-Director-Job-Description.pdf.

Hafiz, Yasmine. "LOOK: 100 Years Of Glorious History From The Hampton Ministers' Conference." *HuffPost*, June 2, 2014. https://www.huffpost.com/entry/hampton-university-ministers-conference_n_5431497.

Hamilton, Victor P. *Handbook on the Pentateuch: Genesis, Exodus, Leviticus, Numbers, Deuteronomy*. Grand Rapids: Baker Academic, 2005.

Hardon, John A. *A Prophet for the Priesthood*. Bardstown, KY: Eternal Life, 1998.

Hartford Institute for Religion Research, The. "Navigating the Pandemic: A First Look at Congregational Responses." Exploring the Pandemic Impact on Congregations, November 2022. https://www.covidreligionresearch.org/research/national-survey-research/navigating-the-pandemic-a-first-look/.

Hendron, Jill Anne, et al. "The Unseen Cost: A Discussion of the Secondary Traumatization Experience of the Clergy." *Pastoral Psychology* 61, no. 2 (2012) 221–31. http://dx.doi.org/10.1007/s11089-011-0378-z.

Howard, Denny. *At Full Strength: Navigating the Risks of Ministry and Vocational Caregiving.* Indianapolis: Wesleyan, 2018.

Hybels, Celia F., et al. "Persistent Depressive Symptoms in a Population with High Levels of Occupational Stress: Trajectories Offer Insights into Both Chronicity and Resilience." *Journal of Psychiatric Practice* 24, no. 6 (2018) 399–409.

International Board of Christian Care. "FAQ." IBCC Global, n.d. https://www.ibccglobal.com/bcctr/faq/. Accessed May 11, 2022.

International Christian Coaching Institute. "Three Levels of Credentialing." ICCI, n.d. https://iccicoaching.com/credentialing/. Accessed May 12, 2022.

Jackson, Debora. *Spiritual Practices for Effective Leadership: 7 Rs of Sanctuary for Pastors.* Valley Forge, PA: Judson, 2015.

Jankowski, Peter J., et al. "Religious Leaders' Well-Being: Protective Influences for Humility and Differentiation Against Narcissism." *Spirituality in Clinical Practice* 9, no. 2 (2022) 103–13.

Jennings, Willie James. *After Whiteness: An Education in Belonging.* Grand Rapids: Eerdmans, 2020.

Jones, Jeffrey M. "U.S. Church Membership Falls Below Majority for First Time." *Gallup*, March 29, 2021. https://news.gallup.com/poll/341963/church-membership-falls-below-majority-first-time.aspx.

Juillard, Helene, et al. "Haiti + 10 Impact Evaluation—Summary." Haiti Learning, n.d. https://haitilearning.alnap.org/system/files/content/resource/files/main/SwS_Impact-Evaluation-Haïti-Executive-Summary.pdf.

Jungclaus, Andrew. "Secularizing Philanthropy in the Twentieth Century: The Pew Family as Trustees of Divine Endowment." *Religions* 9, no. 12 (2018) 380.

Khurana, Mansee. "The Religious Leaders Caught in the Vaccine Wars." *Atlantic*, January 28, 2022. https://www.theatlantic.com/culture/archive/2022/01/religious-leaders-keeping-faith-vaccine/621387/.

King, David P., et al. "The National Study of Congregations' Economic Practices." NSCEP, September 2019. https://www.nscep.org/wp-content/uploads/2019/09/Lake_NSCEP_09162019-F-LR.pdf.

Kirsch, Johann Peter. "Council of Trent." In vol. 15 of *The Catholic Encyclopedia.* New York: Appleton, 1912. https://www.newadvent.org/cathen/15030c.htm.

Kreis, Maria Clara, and Marian K. Diaz. "Factors Cultivating Well-Being of Women Religious in Ministry and Their Resonance with Research on the Workforce." *Journal of Spirituality in Mental Health* (2021) 1–18.

Landau, Elizabeth. "In Haiti, Mental Aftershocks Could Be Far-Reaching." *CNN*, January 19, 2010. http://www.cnn.com/2010/HEALTH/01/15/haiti.mental.psychological.effects/index.html.

Leadership Network. https://leadnet.org/about/.

Lehman, Edward C., Jr. "Gender and Ministry Style: Things Not What They Seem." *Sociology of Religion* 54, no. 1 (1993) 1–11.

Lenski, Noel Emmanuel. *The Cambridge Companion to the Age of Constantine.* Cambridge: Cambridge University Press, 2012.

Lewis, Stephen, et al. *Another Way: Living and Leading Change on Purpose.* St. Louis: Chalice, 2020.

Lifeway Research. "Study of Pastor Attrition and Pastoral Ministry." Lifeway Research, 2021. https://research.lifeway.com/pastorprotection/.

Bibliography

Lilly Endowment Inc. "Grant Guidelines and Procedures." Lilly Endowment, n.d. https://lillyendowment.org/for-grantseekers/guidelines/. Accessed May 13, 2022.

———. "Our Work." Lilly Endowment, n.d. https://lillyendowment.org/our-work/. Accessed May 13, 2022.

———. "Pathways for Tomorrow Initiative." Lilly Endowment, n.d. https://lillyendowment.org/pathways-for-tomorrow-initiative/. Accessed May 9, 2022.

Lilly Family School of Philanthropy. *Giving USA 2021: The Annual Report on Philanthropy for the Year 2020.* Chicago: Giving USA, 2021.

———. "Lake Institute on Faith & Giving to Carry Forward the Legacy of the Ecumenical Stewardship Center." Philanthropy, April 5, 2021. https://philanthropy.iupui.edu/news-events/news-item/lake-institute-on-faith-&-giving-to-carry-forward-the-legacy-of-the-ecumenical-stewardship-center.html?id=353.

Lindsay, D. Michael, and Robert Wuthnow. "Financing Faith: Religion and Strategic Philanthropy." *Journal for the Scientific Study of Religion* 49, no. 1 (2010) 87–111. https://doi.org/10.1111/j.1468-5906.2009.01494.x.

Lipka, Michael. "Many U.S. Congregations Are Still Racially Segregated, but Things Are Changing." Pew Research Center, December 8, 2014. https://www.pewresearch.org/fact-tank/2014/12/08/many-u-s-congregations-are-still-racially-segregated-but-things-are-changing-2/.

Lissner, Will. "Ford Aid Is Given to Negro Clergy." *New York Times*, January 6, 1968.

M. J. Murdock Charitable Trust. "Leadership Now." Murdock Trust, n.d. https://murdocktrust.org/leadership-and-capacity-building/leadership-now/. Accessed May 13, 2022.

MacDonald, G. Jeffrey. "Oldest US Graduate Seminary to Close Campus." *Religion News Service*, November 13, 2015. https://religionnews.com/2015/11/13/oldest-u-s-graduate-seminary-to-close-campus-denominations-secularization-andover-theological/.

Maclellan Foundation Inc., The. https://maclellan.net/about.

Madison, James H. *Eli Lilly: A Life, 1885–1977.* Indianapolis: Indiana Historical Society, 1989.

Marble Retreat. https://marbleretreat.org.

Marrs, Richard. "Christian Counseling: The Past Generation and the State of the Field." *Concordia* 40, no. 1 (2014) 30–36. https://scholar.csl.edu/cgi/viewcontent.cgi?article=1050&context=cj.

Martin, Ralph P., and Peter H. Davids, eds. *Dictionary of the Later New Testament & Its Developments: A Compendium of Contemporary Biblical Scholarship.* Downers Grove, IL: InterVarsity, 1997.

Matthews, Victor Harold, et al. *The IVP Bible Background Commentary: Old Testament.* Downers Grove, IL: InterVarsity, 2000. Electronic ed.

McConnell, Michael W. "Reclaiming the Secular and the Religious: The Primacy of Religious Autonomy." *Social Research* 76, no. 4 (2009) 1340.

Médecins Sans Frontières. "Ten Years after Haiti Earthquake, Medical Care Is Deteriorating." Médecins Sans Frontières, January 9, 2020. https://www.msf.org/ten-years-after-haiti-earthquake-medical-care-deteriorating.

Merton, Thomas. "Spiritual Direction." *Merton Seasonal* 32, no. 1 (2007) 3–17.

Miles, Andrew, and Rae Jean Proeschold-Bell. "Overcoming the Challenges of Pastoral Work? Peer Support Groups and Psychological Distress among United Methodist Church Clergy." *Sociology of Religion* 74, no. 2 (2013) 199–226.

Bibliography

Miller, Emily McFarlan. "Misconduct Allegations against Willow Creek Founder Bill Hybels Are Credible, Independent Report Finds." *Washington Post*, March 1, 2019. https://www.washingtonpost.com/religion/2019/03/01/independent-report-finds-allegations-against-willow-creek-founder-bill-hybels-are-credible/.

Milstein, Glen, et al. "A Prospective Study of Clergy Spiritual Well-Being, Depressive Symptoms, and Occupational Distress." *Psychology of Religion and Spirituality* 12, no. 4 (2020) 409–16.

Ministers and Missionaries Benefit Board. "Timeline." MMBB, n.d. https://www.mmbb.org/why-mmbb/our-story/timeline. Accessed April 11, 2022.

Ministers Fellowship International. https://mfileader.org/about/.

Moore, Edgar. "Ed Moore: Clergy Depression Paralyzes." *Faith & Leadership*, October 7, 2013. https://faithandleadership.com/ed-moore-clergy-depression-paralyzes.

Morrison, Heather. "Wheaton Summit Examines Mental Health and Wellbeing for Clergy." *Religion News Service*, December 6, 2019. https://religionnews.com/2019/12/06/wheaton-summit-examines-mental-health-and-wellbeing-for-clergy/.

Mullin, Robert Bruce. Review of *Hurrying toward Zion: Universities, Divinity Schools, and American Protestantism*, by Conrad Cherry. *Anglican and Episcopal History* 66, no. 3 (1997) 407–10.

Nadolny, Tricia L. "'The Tongue Is a Fire': Southern Baptist Church Fractures over Secrets and Spiritual Abuse." *USA Today*, February 12, 2020. https://www.usatoday.com/in-depth/news/investigations/2020/02/13/southern-baptist-sex-abuse-pastors-history-divided-church/4586698002/.

National Association of United Methodist Foundations. http://naumf.org/.

National Congregations Study. "National Survey of Religious Leaders." National Congregations Study, n.d. https://sites.duke.edu/ncsweb/national-survey-of-religious-leaders-2/.

Nieuwhof, Carey. "29% of Pastors Want to Quit: How to Keep Going When You've Lost Confidence In Yourself." *Carey Nieuwhof* (blog), April 4, 2021. https://careynieuwhof.com/29-of-pastors-want-to-quit-how-to-keep-going-when-youve-lost-confidence-in-yourself/.

Nortey, Justin. "More Houses of Worship Are Returning to Normal Operations, but In-Person Attendance Is Unchanged Since Fall." Pew Research, March 22, 2022. https://www.pewresearch.org/fact-tank/2022/03/22/more-houses-of-worship-are-returning-to-normal-operations-but-in-person-attendance-is-unchanged-since-fall/.

Nouwen, Henri J. M. *In the Name of Jesus: Reflections on Christian Leadership.* Chestnut Ridge, PA: Crossroad, 1992.

———. *The Wounded Healer: Ministry in Contemporary Society.* New York: Doubleday, 1972.

Osborne, Kenan B. *Orders and Ministry: Leadership in the World Church.* Maryknoll, NY: Orbis, 2006.

PastorServe. "Pastor Focused Coaching." PastorServe, n.d. https://pastorserve.org/coaching/. Accessed May 11, 2022.

Pension Fund of the Christian Church. "Excellence in Ministry." Pension Fund, n.d. http://www.pensionfund.org/what-we-offer/excellence-in-ministry. Accessed May 5, 2022.

———. "History." Pension Fund, n.d. http://www.pensionfund.org/about/history. Accessed May 5, 2022.

Peterson, Eugene H. *Working the Angles: The Shape of Pastoral Integrity*. Grand Rapids: Eerdmans, 1987.

Pew Research Center. "America's Changing Religious Landscape." Pew Research, May 12, 2015. https://www.pewresearch.org/religion/2015/05/12/americas-changing-religious-landscape/.

Poole, Shelia. "AME Church Uncovers 'Possible' Irregularities in Retirement Fund." *Atlanta Journal-Constitution*, December 14, 2021.

Presbyterian Foundation. https://www.presbyterianfoundation.org/about-us/.

Proeschold-Bell, Rae Jean, and Jason Byassee. *Faithful and Fractured: Responding to the Clergy Health Crisis*. Grand Rapids: Baker Academic, 2018.

Proeschold-Bell, Rae Jean, and Sara H. LeGrand. "High Rates of Obesity and Chronic Disease among United Methodist Clergy." *Obesity* 18, no. 9 (2010) 1867–70.

Proeschold-Bell, Rae Jean, and Patrick J. McDevitt. "An Overview of the History and Current Status of Clergy Health." *Journal of Prevention & Intervention in the Community* 40, no. 3 (2012) 177–79. https://doi.org/10.1080/10852352.2012.680407.

Proeschold-Bell, Rae Jean, et al. "A 2-Year Holistic Health and Stress Intervention: Results of an RCT in Clergy." *American Journal of Preventive Medicine* 53, no. 3 (2017) 290–99. https://doi.org/10.1016/j.amepre.2017.04.009.

———. "Using Effort-Reward Imbalance Theory to Understand High Rates of Depression and Anxiety among Clergy." *Journal of Primary Prevention* 34, no. 6 (2013) 439–53. https://doi.org/10.1007/s10935-013-0321-4.

Ramachandran, Vijaya, and Julie Walz. "Haiti's Earthquake Generated a $9bn Response— Where Did the Money Go?" *Guardian*, January 14, 2013. https://www.theguardian.com/global-development/poverty-matters/2013/jan/14/haiti-earthquake-where-did-money-go.

Rearden, Myles. "Priesthood, High and Low?" *Furrow* 58, no. 10 (2007) 541–47.

Reber, Robert E., and D. Bruce Roberts, eds. *A Lifelong Call to Learn: Approaches to Continuing Education for Church Leaders*. Nashville: Abingdon, 2000.

Roberts, D. Bruce. "Society for the Advancement of Continuing Education for Ministry (SACEM)—History." Allm, n.d. http://alllm.org/history.html. Site discontinued.

Roberts, Kim. "Global Leadership Network, Formerly Willow Creek Association, Continues Training Church Leaders Around the Country and World—Ministry Watch." Ministry Watch, May 18, 2022. https://ministrywatch.com/global-leadership-network-formerly-willow-creek-association-continues-training-church-leaders-around-the-country-and-world/.

Rockefeller Foundation, The. https://www.rockefellerfoundation.org/about-us/.

Roebuck, David G. "'I Have Done the Best I Could': Opportunities and Limitations for Women Ministers in the Church of God—A Pentecostal Denomination." *Theology Today* 68, no. 4 (January 2012) 393–403. https://doi.org/10.1177/0040573611424794.

"Roman Catholic Church Sex Abuse Cases." *New York Times*, April 16, 2019–June 23, 2022. Collection of articles. https://www.nytimes.com/topic/organization/roman-catholic-church-sex-abuse-cases.

Rose, Kenneth, and Darwin Stapleton. "Toward a 'Universal Heritage': Education and the Development of Rockefeller Philanthropy, 1884–1913." *Teachers College Record* 93, no. 3 (March 1, 1992) 536–55.

Rubenstein, Richard E. *When Jesus Became God: The Epic Fight over Christ's Divinity in the Last Days of Rome*. Boston: Houghton Mifflin Harcourt, 2013.

Ryken, Leland, et al. *Dictionary of Biblical Imagery*. Downers Grove, IL: InterVarsity, 1998.

Bibliography

Sael, Emmanuel, et al. "A Decade after the Earthquake, Haiti Still Struggles to Recover." *Conversation*, January 9, 2020. http://theconversation.com/a-decade-after-the-earthquake-haiti-still-struggles-to-recover-129670.

Scalise, Eric. "What Is Christian Life Coaching?" ICCI Coaching, n.d. https://iccicoaching.com/about/what-is-christian-life-coaching/. Accessed May 12, 2022.

Scazzero, Peter. *Emotionally Healthy Spirituality: Unleash a Revolution in Your Life in Christ*. Nashville: Integrity, 2006.

Schillebeeckx, Edward. *Ministry: Leadership in the Community of Jesus Christ*. New York: Crossroad, 1981.

Schleifer, Cyrus, and Amy D. Miller. "Occupational Gender Inequality among American Clergy, 1976–2016: Revisiting the Stained-Glass Ceiling." *Sociology of Religion* 78, no. 4 (2017–2018) 387–410.

Schürer, Emil. *A History of the Jewish People in the Time of Jesus Christ*. Translated by Sophia Taylor and Peter Christie. Vol. 1. New York: T&T Clark, 1973.

Seim, David L. "Rockefeller Philanthropy and Modern Social Science." Economic History Association, December 2014. https://eh.net/book_reviews/rockefeller-philanthropy-and-modern-social-science/.

Serfass, Adam. "Church Finances from Constantine to Justinian, 312–565 C.E." PhD diss., Stanford University, 2002. https://www.proquest.com/docview/305526909/abstract/129A4A32EFEB4BE4PQ/1.

Shellnutt, Kate. "Southern Baptists Refused to Act on Abuse, Despite Secret List of Pastors." *Christianity Today*, May 22, 2022. https://www.christianitytoday.com/news/2022/may/southern-baptist-abuse-investigation-sbc-ec-legal-survivors.html.

Showers, Vince E., et al. "Charitable Giving Expenditures and the Faith Factor." *American Journal of Economics and Sociology* 70, no. 1 (2011) 152.

Sielaff, Andrea M., et al. "Literature Review of Clergy Resilience and Recommendations for Future Research." *Journal of Psychology and Theology* 49, no. 4 (2021) 308–23.

Silliman, Daniel. "Facing Financial Challenges, TEDS Cuts Faculty Positions." *Christianity Today*, April 12, 2022. https://www.christianitytoday.com/news/2022/april/teds-financial-trouble-crisis-perrin-faculty-cuts.html.

Smietana, Bob. "For Some Pastors, the Past Year Was a Sign from God It Was Time to Quit." *Religion News Service*, May 7, 2021. https://religionnews.com/2021/05/07/for-some-pastors-the-past-year-was-a-sign-that-it-was-time-to-quit/.

———. "More Than $90 Million Missing from AME Pension Funds, Claim Class-Action Lawsuits." *Religion News Service*, April 6, 2022. https://religionnews.com/2022/04/06/more-than-90-million-missing-from-ame-pensions-funds-claim-class-action-lawsuits/.

———. "More Than $90 Million Missing from AME Pension Funds, Lawsuits Claim." *Washington Post*, April 8, 2022. https://www.washingtonpost.com/religion/2022/04/08/ame-pensions-lawsuits/

Smith, Gregory A. "About Three-in-Ten U.S. Adults Are Now Religiously Unaffiliated." Pew Forum, December 14, 2021. https://www.pewforum.org/2021/12/14/about-three-in-ten-u-s-adults-are-now-religiously-unaffiliated/.

Society for the Advancement of Continuing Education for Ministry. "Society for the Advancement of Continuing Education for Ministry (SACEM)—AGM 2015 Minutes." ALLLM, 2015. http://alllm.org/history/agm-2015-minutes.html. Site discontinued.

SOULeader Resources. "Personal, Group & Team Coaching." SOULeader Resrouces, n.d. https://www.souleader.org/personal-coaching. Accessed May 13, 2022.

Stephens-Reed, Laura. "The Coming Tidal Wave of Pastoral Departures." *Laura Stephens-Reed* (blog), September 8, 2020. https://www.laurastephensreed.com/blog/the-coming-tidal-wave-of-pastoral-departures.

Stevenson-Moessner, Jeanne, and Teresa Snorton, eds. *Women Out of Order: Risking Change and Creating Care in a Multicultural World*. Minneapolis: Fortress, 2009.

Stott, John R. W. "Ideals of Pastoral Ministry." In *Vital Ministry Issues: Examining Concerns and Conflicts in Ministry*, edited by Roy B. Zuck, 67–75. Vital Issues. Eugene, OR: Wipf & Stock, 2004.

Taylor, Charles. *A Secular Age*. Cambridge, MA: Harvard University Press, 2009.

Terrell, Kenneth. "AARP Foundation Aims to Recover Church Retirement Funds." AARP, April 4, 2022. https://www.aarp.org/politics-society/advocacy/info-2022/aarp-foundation-lawsuit-ame-church-retirement-funds.html.

Texas Methodist Foundation. "Timeline." TMF, n.d. https://tmf-fdn.org/about/history. Accessed May 19, 2022.

Thriving in Ministry. https://thrivinginministry.org/.

Thurman, Howard. *Jesus and the Disinherited*. New York: Abingdon-Cokesbury, 1949.

Tong, Scott, and Allison Hagan. "'The Rise and Fall of Mars Hill': The Abuses of a Superstar Pastor and Megachurch Ruins Left Behind." *WBUR*, January 20, 2022. https://www.wbur.org/hereandnow/2022/01/20/mars-hill-mark-driscoll-podcast.

Topper, Jakob. "Too Many Pastors Are Falling on Their Own Swords." *Baptist News Global*, August 18, 2020. https://baptistnews.com/article/too-many-pastors-are-falling-on-their-own-swords/.

United Nations. "Rebuilding Haiti: The Post-Earthquake Path to Recovery." *United Nations News*, February 12, 2022. https://news.un.org/en/story/2022/02/1111382.

United States Census Bureau. "American Community Survey, B24124: Detailed Occupation for the Full-Time, Year-Round, Civilian Employed Population 16 Years and Over." U.S. Census Bureau, 2019. https://data.census.gov/.

Vanderweele, Tyler, and Brendan Case. "Empty Pews Are an American Public Health Crisis." *Christianity Today*, October 2021. https://www.christianitytoday.com/ct/2021/november/church-empty-pews-are-american-public-health-crisis.html.

Viéban, Anthony. "Ecclesiastical Seminary." In vol. 13 of *The Catholic Encyclopedia*. New York: Appleton, 1912. https://www.newadvent.org/cathen/13694a.htm.

Vinbury, Naomi. "Cluster Approach: Gaps and Shortcomings in UN Coordination of Humanitarian Actors in Post-Earthquake Haiti and Implications for Policy Concerns of the New Humanitarian School of Thought." Clark University, December 2017. https://commons.clarku.edu/idce_masters_papers/178/.

Volf, Miroslav. *Flourishing: Why We Need Religion in a Globalized World*. New Haven, CT: Yale University Press, 2016.

Walker, Seth. *Faithless*. London: Mardle, 2022.

Wall, K. A. "Direction, Spiritual." In *The New Catholic Encyclopedia*, 2nd ed., 4:759–63. Washington, DC: Catholic University of America, 2003.

Watkins, K. *Christian Theological Seminary, Indianapolis: A History of Education for Ministry*. Zionsville, IN: Guild Press of Indiana, 2001.

Webb, Keith E. *The COACH Model for Christian Leaders: Powerful Leadership Skills for Solving Problems, Reaching Goals, & Developing Others*. New York: James, 2019.

Bibliography

Wespath Benefits and Investments. *2020 Annual Report*. Glenview, IL: Wespath, 2020. https://www.wespath.org/assets/1/7/5671.pdf.

————. "Caring for Those Who Serve." YouTube, September 21, 2021. https://www.youtube.com/watch?v=o_eSWsIbcLw.

————. *Dimensions: Connecting Elements of Well-Being* 3, no. 4 (October–December 2018). https://www.wespath.org/assets/1/7/5255.pdf.

Wuellner, Flora Slosson. *Feed My Shepherds: Spiritual Healing and Renewal for Those in Christian Leadership*. Nashville: Upper Room, 1998.

Zavada, Jack. "Willow Creek Association, Now Global Leadership Network." *Learn Religions*, updated February 12, 2020. https://www.learnreligions.com/willow-creek-association-700130.